GIANTS
LEGENDS OF THE OIL AND GAS INDUSTRY

GIANTS

LEGENDS OF THE OIL AND GAS INDUSTRY

GIANTS
LEGENDS OF THE OIL AND GAS INDUSTRY

Mary Hunt
Ha! Publishing
publisher

Veronica Dye Johnson
author

Evangeline Ehl
creative director

Brandi Williams-Feeler
account executive

Kasey Cox
Michael Horton
Ryan Nims
Molly Robinson
ad design & photography

Hendershot Photography
profile photographer

Hendershot Photography
Mark R. Swindler, Photographer
Yellow Wood Photography
contributing photographers

Ellen Hopkins
contributing author

3527 Billy Hext Road
Odessa, Texas 79765
432-550-7339
www.hapublishing.com

Manufactured in the United States of America.

Printed by Taylor Publishing.

ISBN-13: 978-0-9817695-0-9

SAN: 856-499x

Library of Congress Control Number: 2008933237

Photo courtesy of Mark R. Swindler, Photographer

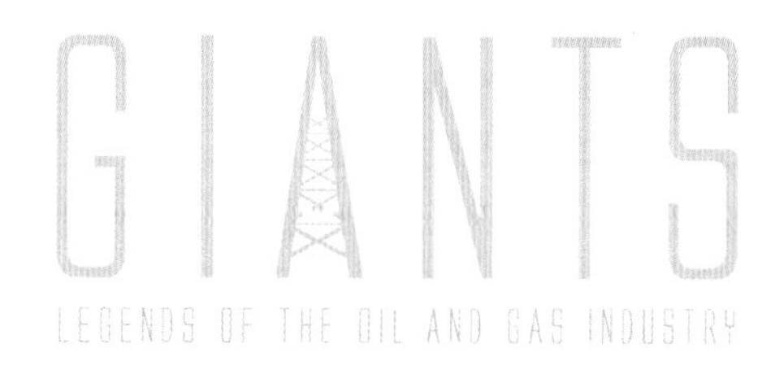

TABLE OF CONTENTS

"Flying the Texas and American flags on a rig is an oil patch tradition." - GIANT Joe Gifford

Photo courtesy of Hendershot Photography

Introduction

The 7 Habits of Highly Effective Oil Men and Women would have been a more appropriate title for this book, but something similar was already taken. (Way to beat me to the punch, Stephen R. Covey.) So, I had to settle for something else that indicated the magnitude of my subjects. *GIANTS*, with its thinly veiled movie allusion, does the job, though I can't help wishing I had coined a new word or phrase for these extraordinary men and women. I considered "ISIs" (Innately Successful Individuals), "Plum-Crazies" (those who lack my healthy fear of failure), and "Dropsies" (people you could drop anywhere in the world, armed only with their moxie, and they'd find a way to thrive). But ultimately I didn't have the patience to push a new word into the modern lexicon.

GIANTS, as they are understood here, are living legends whose activity in the oil and gas industry positively impacts the West Texas community. GIANTS can be found on any part of the industry's spectrum, from exploration to drilling to refining, even to recording the oil patch's history as it happens. GIANTS were by in large chosen by their peers. My contacting of one GIANT would lead to the referral of three more GIANTS, and so on. Each proposed GIANT was checked against such criteria as: a unique story, a reputation of integrity, a remarkable accomplishment, and a philanthropic heart. It should be noted that the selection of GIANTS was not influenced by financial considerations; whether a GIANT bought an ad in this book had no bearing on their inclusion. Simply put, the naming of a GIANT was based on merit alone.

Obviously, there are more GIANTS in West Texas than one book could cover, so for this work (possibly the first in a series) I chose a handful of men and women whose stories balanced nicely with one another. Nick Taylor's affinity for oil histories complements Dr. Diana Hinton's sizeable contribution to the genre. Clayton Williams Jr.'s devil-may-care modus operandi contrasts well with Jim Henry's more reserved approach to risk.

Most people (myself included) find it hard to read through a dry, year-by-year account of a business's growth. Therefore, I've relegated such information to sidebars and devoted the bulk of this book to telling GIANTS' personal anecdotes. My underlying argument is that the qualities that make people successful in business are woven into every aspect of their lives. For example, Dick Saulsbury's recent commitment to exercise and his resultant loss of sixty pounds is just another example of his ability to dedicate himself one-hundred-percent to any goal.

Thank you to all my GIANTS for humoring my inquiries. I know you found it a bit unusual to be asked about your childhood job as a lifeguard or your bungee jumping experience in New Zealand. Previous writers probably asked you more directly how you grew your businesses, but I think my method was more fun.

Veronica Dye Johnson
July 2008

Ernest Angelo peruses the Ronald Reagan section of Odessa, Texas's Presidential Museum while snacking on the former president's favorite finger food. Angelo acted as co-chair for Reagan's Texas-winning Republican Primary campaign in 1976, and as the Texas Primary Chairman and general election Campaign Manager of Reagan's successful second campaign in 1980.

n Events
ury: Ronald Reagan
NANCY DAVIS REAGAN
RONALD REAGAN

Ernest Angelo stands beside a painting of President Reagan and smiles at the memory of Senator John Tower warning him that "supporting Reagan would be the dumbest thing you could do for your political career."

Painting by Cyd Wicker.
The Presidential Museum and Leadership Library in Odessa, Texas.

Ernest Angelo

GIANT POLITICO

"I didn't know at the time that he liked a specific brand: Jelly Bellys," says Ernest Angelo with a touch of regret as he taps the edge of a picture frame. The photograph inside shows Ronald Reagan happily accepting a ribbon-topped jar of jellybeans from a crew-cut-sporting Angelo.

Behind them, the curve-cornered window and cramped seating arrangement indicate that the men are on a plane. Dating from 1976, the photo captures the two en route to a campaign stop. Today, looking at the image of Reagan's broad, iconic smile and laugh-crinkled eyes, Angelo reminisces, "The man himself is what made Reagan successful. He had a great way of communicating his thinking to the people in terms that everyone could understand and identify with. He was very optimistic, positive-thinking, and extremely good at poking fun at himself." This kind of good humor was always present with Reagan: from his joke-sprinkled conversations to his fun choice of Jelly Belly candy.

Angelo walks over to another framed photograph and his face brightens even more. It's an image of the Oval Office. From his Presidential chair, Reagan is exchanging a delighted grin with Angelo, who is seated at his side. On the bottom of the photo is an inscription. Angelo, his eyes twenty-six years older than at the time of the picture, relies on his eyeglasses to read: *Dear Ernie, thanks for all you did to see we could sit in these chairs. Warm regards, Ronald Reagan*. Angelo beams and says, "I'm probably prouder of that than anything else that's happened to me in the political arena."

The year the Oval Office picture was taken, 1982, Angelo's life hadn't been all smiles. That year the Midlander ran for the Texas State Senate and, like his 1968 bid for the same position, lost. Having already helped campaign Reagan into the White House, Angelo knew more than a little bit about winning votes. The problem, as Angelo sees it retrospectively, was an opponent whose platform was almost indistinguishable from his own. Recalls Angelo, "My opponent tended to agree with me on all the issues. I couldn't point out anything significant where we differed. To win, you have to define yourself with something more than just personality, and I couldn't make it happen."

Dear Ernie, thanks for all you did to see we could sit in these chairs. Warm regards, Ronald Reagan.

The senate losses, though disappointing, ultimately did little to dampen a political career as distinguished as Angelo's. A long career as well, it started in 1964 when Angelo volunteered to run a campaign for underdog candidate Bill Keel. Keel was attempting to wrest the Midland County Sheriff's office from Ed Darnell, who had held the post for forty years. The situation looked tough for Keel. It also looked tough for Angelo, who had just gone independent in the oil industry and had three kids, ages four and under. Despite these unpromising odds, Keel, with Angelo's help, threw himself into the race and captured over forty percent of the vote. It wasn't enough to depose Darnell, but Angelo still considers

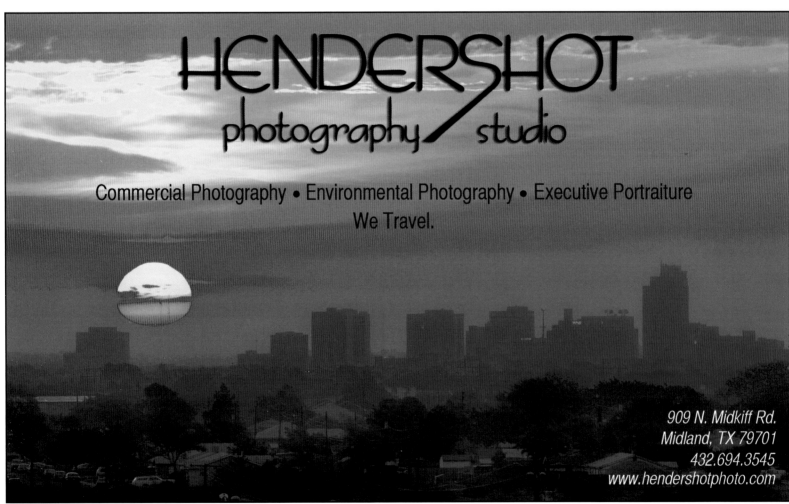

CAREER HIGHLIGHTS

1956 Graduates from Louisiana State University with degree in petroleum engineering; takes job with Gulf in Crane, TX, lives in nearby Odessa, TX

1958 Transferred by Gulf to Midland, TX

1962-1964 Works for Sohio Petroleum

1964 Goes independent as sole proprietor

1970 Joins Don Sparks in Discovery Operating; becomes investment partner in Discovery Exploration

1972 Elected Mayor; sells Discovery Operating interests to Sparks; continues Discovery Exploration investment partnership with Webb Farish

1975 Builds office, which he co-owns with Jim Henderson

1976 State co-chair of Reagan's Texas Primary campaign

1976-1996 Serves as the Republican National Committee Man for Texas for five consecutive terms

1978 Helps form Montero Operating

1980 Chairman of Reagan's second Texas campaign for the presidency

1985 Helps form another operating company, Enerstar Oil & Gas

1997 Appointed by Governor George W. Bush to the Texas Parks and Wildlife Commission

2001-2003 Serves as Vice Chairman of the Texas Parks and Wildlife Commission

2005 Appointed Chairman of the Department of Public Safety Commission by Governor Rick Perry

2006 Angelo removes himself fully from the oil and gas operating business; continues as managing partner of Discovery Exploration

it to have been a "good, hard campaign and a forerunner of what was to come as we worked to change Midland's governing philosophy from Democrat to Republican."

Eight years later, in 1972, Angelo found himself in a considerably better position for political involvement. His sole proprietorship had developed into a stable, growing business and he was an investment partner in several successful companies. Still, the idea of seeking public office did not dawn on him until a fateful luncheon with several Republican friends was held for the purpose of finding a mayoral candidate. In the course of conversation, Angelo jokingly made a deal with buddy Frank Cahoon, saying, "If you'll run for city council, then I'll run for mayor." To Angelo's surprise, Cahoon took the challenge and Angelo found himself running for office. Angelo recalls proudly, "We ran a spirited campaign and had a record turnout of voters." Feeling confident on the election night, Angelo and his supporters were shocked to hear they had lost the mayoral race by 350 votes. Laughing in retrospect at his reaction, Angelo recounts, "I was gonna make my Dick-Nixon-type speech—'You won't have Dick Nixon to kick around anymore.'" But fortunately a friend intervened, begging Angelo not to hold a press conference until he could talk him out of any hasty remarks. Angelo, bitter and ready to bury his political career, grudgingly agreed to stay quiet for a few hours. Around eleven o'clock that night, the candidate's close friend and campaign manager, Bob Monaghan, told him the reported outcome had been incorrect. Instead of losing by 350 votes, Angelo had won by 150. "My kids had already cried and gone to bed by the time we found out I won," remembers the former mayor, chuckling. Having nearly sabotaged himself with a premature press conference, Angelo came to a wise conclusion: "When you're upset and you write a hot letter, it's better to wait and send it the next day."

Angelo served four two-year terms as Midland's mayor. One of his first actions was to expedite city council

▶ Thomas M. Tucker

Tucker Valve Seat Company

Tucker Valve Seat Company is a full-line U.S. manufacturer of valve seat inserts. Tucker Valve Seats are used by original engine manufacturers and some of the world's largest rebuilders of automotive and industrial engines. The company's preeminence in valve seat manufacturing comes from its large inventory and its ability to produce the highest quality machineable product.

The company was started in 1957 after the Tucker family noted the need for a specialized valve seat insert. But no business, not even one filling an obvious market void, has an easy start. When Thomas Tucker returned from military service, he joined his parents in building the family business. In the company's early years, what little sleep Thomas got was caught in bits and pieces at his office while struggling to make ends meet. Eventually, his dedication paid off. The company incorporated in 1971. By 1978, the company's clientele had expanded from regional to international markets.

Tucker valve seats are used in all industries: automotive, locomotive, marine, diesel and natural gas. Tucker Valve Seat Company's success comes from its ability to balance mass production with meeting industries' needs for customized products. The company's customer service department has years of technical service and prides itself on excellent on-time delivery

Thomas Tucker, past president and CEO of Tucker Valve Seat Company, was dedicated to his employees and making his company a success. On January 27, 2008, just five months after his company's fifty-year anniversary, Thomas Martin Tucker passed away. The high standards he set for quality and service persist today, giving Tucker Valve Seat Company the ethical edge in today's global market.

Celebrating 50 Years of Business

Ad designed by Hunt Advertising

meetings by working closely with the city manager to implement a more efficient agenda. Angelo explains, "I didn't want to waste people's money. The city was nearly broke at the time and things were not good. My first year as mayor, we passed the city sales tax and that put Midland on a sound financial footing." The former mayor also takes pride in the Midland Center, new Central Fire Station, and first full remodeling of the Midland airport terminal, all of which were accomplished during his eight years of leadership. Noting that he also oversaw multiple cuts in property taxes, leaving office with Midland boasting the lowest tax rate of the top twenty-five largest Texas cities, Angelo concludes, "Being mayor was a satisfying experience. You actually can have an impact on the direction the city takes."

"Being mayor was a satisfying experience. You actually can have an impact on the direction the city takes."

Though known to Midlanders as a local leader, Angelo has made a name for himself in state and national politics as well. From 1976 to 1996, in five consecutive four-year terms, Angelo acted as the Republican National Committee Man for Texas. In 1997, Governor George W. Bush appointed Angelo to the Texas Parks and Wildlife Commission. An avid hunter and fisherman, Angelo eventually found himself named Vice Chairman of the Commission. Then, in 2005, the state gave Angelo another bid of confidence when Governor Rick Perry appointed him Chairman of the Department of Public Safety Commission.

Reflecting on his simultaneous careers in politics and oil, Angelo observes, "If I couldn't have made a living in the oil business, I wouldn't have been able to do the politics." Laughing, he adds, "Probably the politics, at times, jeopardized my income from the oil business, but I've never regretted the political involvement." What dismays Angelo is not the thought of potential profits lost, but the idea of potential leaders lost because good people won't get involved. He laments, "A lot of people think that being in politics is a bad thing—that it's just dirty pool all the way. What you've got to realize is it's just human nature and you run into the same thing everywhere." To still-dubious citizens, Angelo offers the following rebuttal: "Don't tell me you haven't had situations in Little League or Boy Scouts, or even church-related organizations, where the parents, coaches, or members said or did things that were out-of-line or worse." Angelo finishes emphatically, "If people would realize that there are good and bad elements to politics and government—but only as much as there are good and bad elements to everything we humans do—they'd be more likely to get involved."

Odessa, TX District
David Boggs, Manager
432.617.0114

Midland, TX
Mike Lewter, Jerry Walton
432.617.3018

Hobbs, NM District
Kevin Tate, Sales
432.556.5872

SAFETY
We proudly maintain an excellent safety record.

STABILITY
Rising Star is locally owned by Clyde Hinton and Mike Laferney.

COMPREHENSIVENESS
We conduct independent lab testing for both cementing and acidizing fluids.

CONSISTENCY
Our Cement Batch Plant yields consistent Poz blends with Class C & H, weighing all additives accurately.

PRECISION
Our Batch Mix Control Panel ensures precise and repeatable blends of cement additives.

SERVICE
We provide quality services to majors and independents in West Texas and Southeast New Mexico.

DEDICATION
Our personnel, nearly one-hundred strong, are dedicated to providing services in a safe, precise manner.

Ad designed by Hunt Advertising.

OILFIELD FISHING & RENTAL TOOLS

7111 Andrews Hwy. • Odessa, TX • 432-339-0411

Hinton Enterprises, an Odessa-based fishing & rental tool company, offers customized solutions to common downhole problems. Founded in 1993, Hinton Enterprises has built a reputation for rapid response and comprehensive service.

The Hinton Enterprises team consists of twenty employees, including three workover and completion foremen. The company offers a wide variety of fishing tools and has six reverse units.

David Arrington prepares to capture his favorite subject, his family, in Midland, Texas's Art & Soul dance studio. In the background, wife Shelley readies daughter Amy for her photo while younger sister Katy Grace patiently awaits her turn in the spotlight. Arrington's eldest daughter, Ellen, and son, DJ, (standing off-camera) pitch in as photographer assistants.

Arrington likes to make pilgrimages to places immortalized by Ansel Adams's view camera. Here, Arrington poses with his own view camera.

David H. Arrington

GIANT SHUTTERBUG

Leafing through David H. Arrington's 1979 yearbook, one gathers the oilman was Justin F. High School's most involved senior ever. There's Arrington grinning goofily amongst the Math Club members. Turn the page. There he is again, looking studious on the Debate Team. Turn the page. Arrington trunked up for the Swim Team—How did he find the time?

And, why would a school of 2,500 students rest its hopes for academic and athletic glory so heavily on just one?—There's Arrington donning a beret for the French Club. Turn the page. Oh, here's the Girls' Volleyball Team—well, at least he won't—wait—Arrington's there, too—in the background—peeking roguishly around the gymnasium door! Turn the page. Arrington in the Poetry Club—Arrington hamming it up with the Drama Department—and, finally, turn the page—Arrington as a Yearbook Photographer. Suddenly, everything is hilariously clear: long before Photoshop became a verb, there was a laborious darkroom way to manipulate pictures, and David H. Arrington was one of its practitioners. "That was a lot of hard work!" recalls Arrington, chuckling, "I inserted myself seamlessly into every photo." His gag wasn't discovered until weeks later when the annual staff received their proof books. Predictably, the teachers made Arrington restore the layout's original photos. But undoing his handiwork didn't really bother Arrington; he was still reveling in the fact that there'd always be a handful of legitimate-looking proofs floating around, bearing his alternate take on history.

Only an experienced photographer could have performed such a skill-intensive prank

Only an experienced photographer could have performed such a skill-intensive prank and, by his eighteenth year, Arrington was no amateur. He had been practicing photography for four years, ever since a dull Christmas party prompted him to slip away from the crowd and snoop through his host's home. Coming upon a door that led presumably to the garage, the boy ducked inside and flipped a switch. The resultant red glow revealed rows of strange bottles, stacks of developing trays, and strands of drip-dried photographs. It was the darkroom of Bob Phillips. Today, Phillips is known to television viewers as the Texas Country Reporter, but in 1974 he was known to Arrington simply as the husband of his junior high teacher Mrs. Phillips.

Fortunately, Bob Phillips was pleased rather than peeved when he discovered Arrington's intrusion. He even invited the youth back the next weekend for a photography tutorial. But after just a few rudimentary lessons from the TV personality, the precocious Arrington felt he could learn the rest on his own. With characteristic aplomb, the teen set to developing and marketing his newfound passion and soon won a wedding commission. In retrospect, the oilman has a theory why that first couple entrusted their nuptial photos to a fifteen-year-old boy, "They were probably poor and couldn't afford a *real* photographer." He then hastens to add, "but I'm good, though!" Apparently, he was quite good because the jobs came rolling in and so did the money. Even better, the

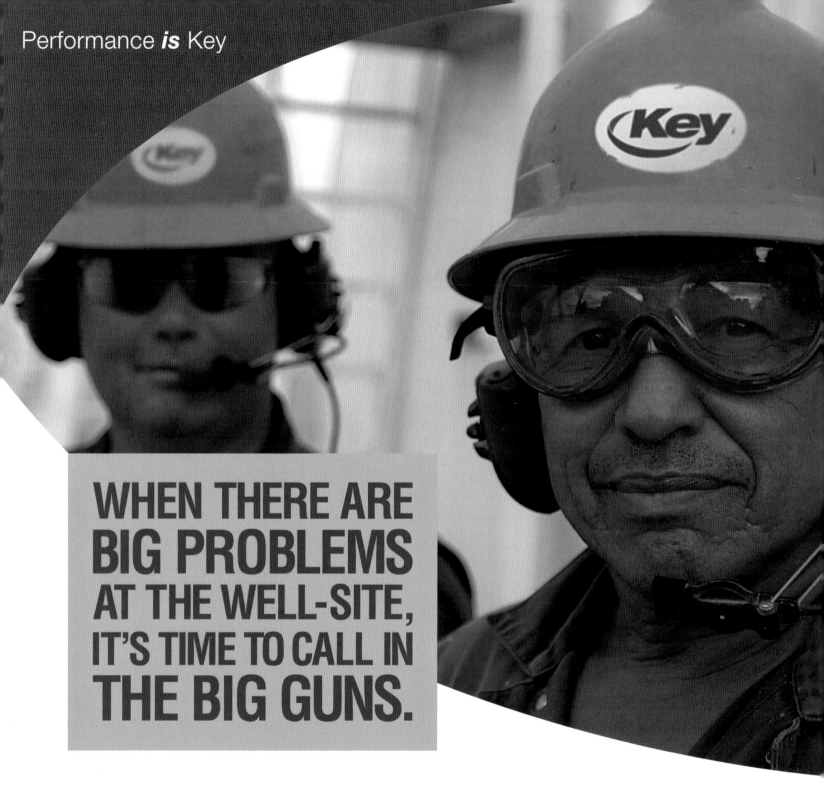

CAREER HIGHLIGHTS

1984 Makes first deal turning a lease in Winkler County, TX

1987 At twenty-seven years old, drills a two hundred barrels/day well in Sterling County's Credo field, sells his stake; makes his first million dollars

1989 Drills ten wells inside Kermit, TX city limits, sells properties

1993 Drills Monument Abo field extension/discovery with each well yielding one thousand barrels a day

2003 Buys his first lease in the Barnett Shale

2004 Drills the third horizontal well in Barnett Shale in Johnson County, TX

2004-2008 Sells partial interest in Barnett Shale to Chesapeake and XTO

2008 Drills his hundredth well in the Barnett Shale

profit margin was high because the teen ran a rather Spartan operation. "I had a darkroom in the bathroom," Arrington laughs. "My parents were very understanding!" Of course, what parents wouldn't encourage their child's after-school business if, as Arrington's did, it provided enough money for their child's first car?

As a high-school senior in Dallas, Texas, Arrington debated whether to follow his older brother to Texas Tech or attend an art school in Los Angeles. Today, Arrington can't remember if he was accepted by the latter, though he's pretty sure he was. "There are a lot of people that accepted me that shouldn't have," he jokes. Turning thoughtful, Arrington muses, "If I had gone out to L.A.—who knows? I might've become—Who was that guy that made Star Wars?—George Lucas. I might've become a George Lucas." On the lips of anyone else, this sentence would sound sarcastic, but Arrington is dead-serious. Throughout his life, the oilman's shown a Rumpelstiltskinian knack for spinning raw materials into riches.

At Texas Tech, Arrington funded his education with photography gigs. Ironically, he had more success with his entrepreneurial pursuits than his studies. His grades were unimpressively average in every class but one. Recalls Arrington proudly, "I wrecked the curve for the kids in the Oil & Gas Accounting class." Consequently, by the time he graduated in 1983, Arrington had no doubt where his future lay. He applied to every oil company in the phone book. But, unfortunately, the bottom had just fallen out of the formerly robust petroleum market and most West Texas companies were jettisoning their staff. Arrington stubbornly ignored the ominous unemployment trend and headed to the Permian Basin. Defending the rationality of his move, Arrington shrugs and says, "I was committed." Then he grins impishly and shares one of his favorite stories, "Out of school, I had twenty-seven job interviews and I had twenty-eight rejections—Getty Oil sent me two rejection letters!" Finally, a company in Andrews, Texas, agreed to take the graduate on, but for a paltry $900 a month. Arrington once again found himself shooting weddings on weekends, this time to subsidize a real-world education in the oil field.

In 1984, after a strenuous year of straddling two jobs, Arrington gratefully obtained a signature loan from Alan B. White (now CEO and

Chairman of PlainsCapital Bank). The $20,000 loan was to cover living expenses only, not investments. Arrington explains, "I told [White] I would take the $20,000 and, if at the end of one year I couldn't show him how I was going to pay him back [through oil deals], I would stop what I was doing, earn $20,000 to pay him back, and then [borrow] it all over again." As it turned out, Arrington wouldn't even need a year. Within ninety days as an independent oil investor, he turned a deal that enabled him to reimburse White and have a hefty grubstake left over to start David H. Arrington Oil & Gas Inc.

Just three years later, at age twenty-seven, Arrington made his first million. Showing a good head for business, the young man folded the money back into his company to acquire more land and employees. The profits of each subsequent deal were applied the same way, as fertilizer to grow the company's assets. Then, in 1993, the oilman's company made a field extension and discovery that resulted in six wells, which each yielded one thousand barrels a day. Arrington felt he could finally afford to spend some of his earnings more creatively—and on creative objects. He began transmuting his excess fortune into a world-class art collection.

In 2007, Arrington's staff presented the oilman with a most unusual gift: bobbleheads created in his likeness.

Ansel Adams is Arrington's favorite photographer. The oilman explains his fascination with the artist this way: "I became a fan for two reasons: One, is the same reason I believe he's the most popular photographer to have ever lived—because his images are remarkable. Two, because of his genius zone system." The zone system is a method of photography Adams developed with fellow teacher Fred Archer around 1940 to help their students at the Art Center School in Los Angeles. The zone system's scale consists of nine values labeled with roman numerals and graded from Zone I (pure black) to Zone IX (base white of the photo paper). The system enables photographers to pre-visualize the photo they're about to take, then adjust the film's exposure and development to produce the desired levels of contrast, value, and detail.

Adams is best known for his dramatic documentations of the American landscape, particularly Yosemite National Park:

FROM THE CROWN
The
Premium
Supplier
to the
Oil & Gas
Industry
SPECIALIZING IN
PRODUCTION
&
DRILLING
BRIDGES
EQUIPMENT LTD.
432-333-9741
ODESSA ★ TEXAS
TO THE GROUND

Zeus-sized thunderclouds menacing a snow-capped mountain, searing white dogwood petals punctuating pitch-dark rock, diaphanous mist wafting up from a pounding waterfall. These majestic images have become a staple of corporate-America décor, but few businessmen sit in their offices each day surrounded by the originals as Arrington does. *Monolith, Face of Half Dome*; *Moonrise, Hernandez*; *Clearing Winter Storm*; *Golden Gate Before the Bridge*—they transform Arrington's office walls into a stunning, black-and-white panorama. And if the visual value of these works were not remarkable enough, there's their art historical value to consider: The 1943 *Moonrise, Hernandez* hanging in Arrington's office, for example, was deemed by Adams to be the most successful of all the prints developed from that negative. Prior to Arrington's acquisition, it hung for decades in Adams's own Yosemite home.

Arrington's confidence as an unofficial Adams historian comes as much from empirical knowledge as book-knowledge. The oilman has made many pilgrimages to the sites immortalized by Adams's view camera. Once there, Arrington has endeavored to duplicate Adams's originals as closely as possible. And, though he can't perfectly recreate an image taken a half-century earlier, just walking in the other man's footsteps has yielded much insight into the artist's method and style. Arrington remarks humbly, "He picked some pretty good places. I figured I couldn't improve on that a whole lot."

"I'm a photographer trapped in an oilman's body."

Arrington's goal has always been to build "the greatest and largest Ansel Adams collection in the world—outside of the University of Arizona's archive."* Over the past fifteen years, he's amassed six hundred different original Adams images. Now that he considers his mission accomplished, he wants to share his passion with others. To this end, the collector has purchased a historic building in Santa Fe, adjacent to the Georgia O'Keefe Museum, to permanently house his collection. The as-yet unnamed museum will feature rotating displays on three stories and a fourth-story "Moonrise" room devoted to multiple iterations of the famous Adams image. With the institution, Arrington intends "to showcase Ansel's work—the whole man." The collector explains, "Everyone thinks he's only a landscape photographer, but he's done a lot of other things." Something quite similar could be said of Arrington. Everyone thinks he's an oilman but, as Arrington brightly puts it, "I'm a photographer trapped in an oilman's body."

* *The Ansel Adams Archive at the Center for Creative Photography at the University of Arizona is the largest repository of Adams's work.*

KB2 INDUS

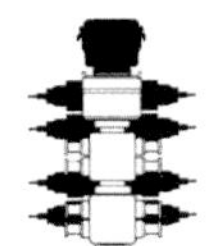

BOP MACHINE

2140 WEST 42ND STREET □ BOX 12430
ODESSA, TEXAS 79768

TRIES, INC.

The definition of "GIANT" is unusually large enterprise.

The Permian Basin serves as headquarters for KB2 Industries, which manufactures blowout preventers (BOPs) and replacement parts, accumulators, and repairs other manufacturers' equipment for the drilling and well service industry.

KB2 INDUSTRIES INC. is the parent company of Melco Blowout Preventer Specialties, Burnsco Blowout Preventer Sales & Services, Townsend International BOPs, BOP Machine, Stressco, Alllbright Machine & HiTech Inc. Ken Burns II, a native West Texan, is President and CEO of KB2 Industries. Ken began building his dream of becoming a major blowout preventer manufacturer in 1975 with the introduction of Melco Blowout Preventer Specialties which manufactures over 4,000 different replacement parts for the major blowout preventer manufacturers such as Cameron, Shaffer and Hydril.

In 1980, Ken introduced Burnsco Blowout Preventer Sales & Services to address the local demand for repairs to blowout preventers and accumulators. There is only a handful of repair facilities in the United States that performs this task. In 2000, Burnsco received its API (American Petroleum Institute) certification to manufacture blowout preventers, accumulators and other component parts. Burnsco also introduced the "Bison" Accumulator product line in late 2002 and manufactures accumulators for both the drilling and well service industry.

In 1990, Ken purchased Allbright Machine, which has been established for over 50 years, for the purpose of manufacturing blowout preventer replacement parts. To Ken's surprise, Allbright also had a product line that serviced the oil industry, which included products for the well service industry such as swab mandrels, tube jars, rope sockets and ball guns used when fracing.

In 2000, Ken expanded his operations to Oklahoma City to include a general machine shop that repairs different component parts on drilling rigs such as rotary tables, swivels, elevators and draw-works. This operation also included blowout preventer repair, which piqued Ken's interest. HiTech has become a support group for the repair of larger component parts on blowout preventers.

In 2000, Ken also developed BOP Machine, in Odessa, Texas, for the specific purpose of specializing in the correct repair and rebuild of large blowout preventer bodies. The development of Stressco, a stress relief facility, followed shortly afterwards to address stress relief after welding on the large body parts.

In 2002, Ken came closer to accomplishing his dream of becoming a major player in the blowout preventer manufacturing business with the acquisition of Townsend Machine & Supply, which manufactured a line of well service blowout preventers. Ken immediately changed the name to Townsend International BOPs and began manufacturing the larger preventers for the drilling industry. Ken has expanded his product line to include preventers that are comparable with Cameron, Shaffer and Hydril, making Townsend "The NAPA store for blowout preventers."

KB2 Industries continues to expand by developing a 29 acre complex beginning at 2140 S. County Road W. in Odessa, Texas to better serve the drilling and well service industry. For more information contact us at www.melcobop.com, www.burnscobop.com and www.townsendbops.com.

MELCO BLOWOUT PREVENTER SPECIALTIES INC.

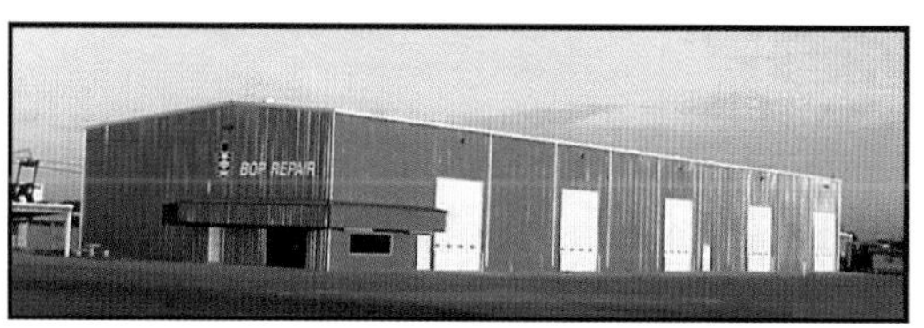

BURNSCO BLOWOUT PREVENTER SALES & SERVICES INC.

TOWNSEND INTERNATIONAL BOPS INC.

BOP MACHINE

ALLBRIGHT MACHINE

HITECH MACHINE INC.

Ice
BLOCKBUSTER VIDEO

"Driving 42nd street is more dangerous than well firefighting," opines Ace Barnes as he surveys one of Odessa, Texas's most treacherous thoroughfares.

Ace Barnes

GIANT COMPOSURE

Ace Barnes contends that driving 42nd Street in Odessa, Texas, is more dangerous than fighting oil well fires. And, surprisingly enough, statistics are on his side. In 2007 alone, 42nd Street had two fatalities and eight incapacitating crashes out of 237 total collisions.*

By contrast, there have been only two fatalities over *thirty years* on the approximately five hundred fires Barnes has fought. The paradoxical truth is that the safest time to be around a well is when it's on fire because by then it's predictable—most of the time.

A. C. "Ace" Barnes began firefighting at age forty-nine as the first employee of Boots & Coots, an international well control company. The eponymous E. O. "Coots" Matthews had met Barnes several years earlier, when Barnes was working as a drilling mud engineer and Coots was putting out fires for the Red Adair Company. At the time, Coots had observed with interest the mud-man's cool head and wise actions. When Coots and his coworker Asger "Boots" Hansen left Adair to form their own company, they knew just whom to recruit.

The safest time to be around a well is when it's on fire.

Barnes signed on with Boots & Coots on January 4, 1978. Just eight days later, the engineer was on a plane bound for Bolivia and his first firefighting assignment. It wasn't exactly a jetsetter's lifestyle, but the engineer had never even been outside the U.S. before and suddenly he was traveling the world. It was exciting. However, Barnes quickly discovered that flying *to* a job and flying *from* a job could be two very different experiences. "If [the well owners] are in a big hurry, they'll send a charter plane for you. But once you get there, they don't care how you get home," Barnes comments wryly.

No matter where in the world a well fire erupts, it always requires the same work sequence. First, the rig and other debris must be dragged from the inferno and extinguished. Clearing out the area restricts the fire to a more manageable, vertical path. The columnar blaze is then drenched with water pumped from a nearby ditch or line of five-hundred-barrel tanks. If water fails to quench the fire, dynamite is brought in to "shoot the well out." This detonation of dynamite snuffs out the conflagration by interrupting its oxygen supply.

The most time-consuming part of putting out a well fire is clearing out the melted rig. Because the wells in Kuwait were already producers when they were ignited in 1991, there were no rigs to remove. Thus, Barnes recalls, the firefighters were often able to put out two wells in one day. After a well fire is extinguished, the entire site is scoured for smoldering debris that could start another blaze. Once the area has been checked out, old equipment on the well head is replaced with new.

CAREER HIGHLIGHTS

1949 Moves from Rockwall, TX to Kermit, TX to work for Rowan Drilling Co.

1955 Works for Baroid as a drilling mud engineer

1977 Starts own drilling mud business, Ace Mud Co.

1978 Hired as first employee of Boots & Coots International Well Control Inc.

1991 Spends 160 days putting out fires in Kuwait

2000 Oil market downturn forces closing of Ace Mud Co.

2008 Barnes, at seventy-nine years old, is still fighting well fires

An exception to this firefighting sequence comes when a locale is inadequately equipped, or when the equipment is available but there's no route to transport it to the fire. For example, of the 161 days Barnes and crew spent putting out well fires from the Gulf War, twenty-five elapsed just building a road to reach Kuwait's biggest well. Setbacks like these were inconvenient, but still not stressful enough to disquiet Barnes.

In fact, there's only one incident in his thirty-year firefighting career that Barnes admits was nerve-wracking—unloading a fifty-five-gallon drum of dynamite that had failed to ignite inside a well fire. Coots and Barnes had been attempting to shoot out a particularly stubborn blaze when something unusual happened: the dynamite wouldn't ignite. There it was, a fifty-five-gallon drum's worth of explosives, dangling at the end of an eighty-foot boom into the heart of the well fire, and nothing was happening. Hoping it was the dynamite caps that were faulty, Coots and Barnes changed out the batteries. Nothing. They changed the batteries again. And again. No explosion.

Thinking perhaps persistence was the solution, they left the dynamite in the fire and waited. It still didn't ignite.

They shot at the explosives with a rifle. Still nothing.

Coots turned to Barnes grimly, "You know what that means don't you?" Barnes looked around the desolate site. "Yeah, where are all of our helpers?" he asked with mock ruefulness. But, internally, Barnes knew it had been wise to send the other workers home after the dynamite's first failure. This was too risky of a situation for an entire crew's exposure.

Resolving themselves to the unenviable task, Coots and Barnes climbed into the boom truck. Delicately, they dragged the eighty-foot boom with its volatile parcel out of the inferno. And, for the first time all day, Coots and Barnes were thrilled with the dynamite's unresponsiveness. The extricated explosives were, by all indications, defective, but the firefighters didn't take any chances. They inundated the pile with hundreds of gallons of water. Not until this final precaution was executed did the two men feel secure.

"As long as I can point my finger."

In 2008, Barnes celebrated his thirtieth year with Boots & Coots. He is the oldest active Senior Well Control Specialist. Fortunately for Barnes, there's no pressure to quit the job he loves. For one thing, well firefighting hasn't changed much. Sure, with today's technology, wells are a bit less likely to blow out: pressure can be anticipated and countered with weighted mud. But there are still enough surprise blowouts to keep Barnes busy. Plus, unlike some industries where the knowledge of seasoned workers is written off as obsolete, Barnes's wisdom is well-valued in the oil field. "First-time firefighters are agitated, excited," Barnes explains. "They need a pat on the back [from me] that gives assurance and calms them down." When asked how long he plans to direct the snuffing of well fires, Barnes answers confidently, "As long as I can point my finger."

** These figures were supplied by the Texas Department of Transportation with the caveat that the data was preliminary and incomplete. At the time of* GIANTS' *publication, these numbers had not been finalized or certified.*

Longtime Summer Mummers volunteer **Arlen Edgar** discovers even grunt work can be glamorous when some lovely assistants show up. Fresh from their hip-shimmying Mummers number, The Aloha O-Hawaii dance troupe of Midland (l-r: Jane Dagdag, Marichu Manley, and Denise Kepple) proves they can pitch popcorn with the best of them.

Arlen L. Edgar

GIANT PATRON

Arlen L. Edgar seats himself at a fake piano and begins jauntily pantomiming to Patsy Cline's classic "I Fall to Pieces." His gartered arms pump vigorously up and down. His fingers twiddle across the painted keys. His old-timey skimmer hat slides rakishly over one ear. Before him, a dazzling chanteuse sexily mouths the lyrics with bright red lips.

As the song's chorus approaches, Edgar surreptitiously switches to one-handed playing so he can pluck an invisible string. Whoosh! The singer's fake, mannequin arms fall right off her sequin-clad body. The audience roars with delight. Another chorus, another string pull, and the woman's wig flies away. And so it goes till the singer has literally fallen to pieces. Arlen Edgar and the now-limbless lady grin and bow beneath a shower of popcorn.

Edgar's eyes twinkle as he recalls the performance over two decades later. "That was a lot of fun," he chuckles. The petroleum engineer had penned the skit himself as part of the Olio, a medley of dance and comedy routines that follow the melodrama in a Summer Mummers production for Midland Community Theatre. Summer Mummers, dreamt up in 1949 as a fundraiser for a fledgling playhouse in Midland, Texas, is now the longest-running summer theatre in the state. It is also the most bawdy and butter-filled. Each year, a local author composes an original script to be performed by a big-eyed Damsel, a moustache-twirling Villain, a hunky Hero, and other clichéd characters. Melodrama at its maximum, every line elicits boos or cheers from the beer-swilling audience.

Summer Mummers is the most bawdy and butter-filled summer theatre in Texas.

Summer Mummers, with its season-long schedule, requires several hundred volunteers a year. In the 1970s, Arlen Edgar and his wife, Betty, volunteered as house managers. Summer Mummers had not yet found its home in the Yucca Theatre and was being held in the local American Legion Hall. As Edgar recounts, "A lot of funny things happened there. The roof leaked when it rained. The rain would fall on the hardwood floors, which were saturated with popcorn oil." The result was a surface "slick as glass, with people falling all over the place." Edgar laughs, "It was very exciting." The Edgars' sons, who were ten- and twelve-years-old at the time, tagged along and set up chairs. Though the work was dull, the sights, smells, and sounds of Summer Mummers were more than enough compensation. "They had the best time you can imagine," says Edgar. When the family of four arrived home after a long Mummers evening, their skin and hair were permeated with popcorn oil. Buttery kernels spilled from every article of clothing.

When out-of-town friends came for a visit, Edgar delighted in taking them to Summer Mummers. He'd start his tour with the theatre's backside. "What the cast people remember from that era was there were no dressing rooms. The cast had to change in cars in the alley." There by a dumpster would be the tall, imposing villain affixing his

L&S
EQUIPMENT

CAREER HIGHLIGHTS

1957 Graduates with BS in petroleum engineering from the University of Texas at Austin

1957-1961 Junior, Intermediate Engineer with Pan American Petroleum Corporation (now Amoco)

1961-1967 Reservoir Engineer and Manager of Consulting Division for Leibrock, Landreth, Campbell and Callaway, Consulting Petroleum Engineers (now Williamson Petroleum Consultants); also a Director of Kanata Exploration Company of Canada

1967-1971 Successively, Vice President, President, and Director of Tipperary Land and Exploration; Managing Director of Tipperary in Australia

1971-1973 General Manager of Western States Producing Company

1973-Present Independent oil investor and petroleum consultant

1981 Named Distinguished Graduate by University of Texas's College of Engineering; Named Engineer of the Year by Permian Basin chapter of Society for Petroleum Engineers (SPE); President of Society of Petroleum Engineers

1986 President of American Institute of Mining, Metallurgical and Petroleum Engineers

1992 President of Society of Petroleum Evaluation Engineers

1993-Present Trustee of the Abell-Hanger Foundation

1995-1997 Director of SIPES National (Society of Independent Professional Earth Scientists)

1996 SIPES President

2001 Named with wife, Betty, Distinguished Arts Volunteers for 2000-2001 by Arts Assembly of Midland, TX

2004 Receives Top Hand Award from Permian Basin Petroleum Association

2008 Receives Lifetime Achievement Award from Hearst Energy Awards

handlebar moustache with spirit gum. The wigless damsel would be stepping gingerly into a voluminous petticoat. The hero's hayseed sidekick would be dotting his cheeks with eyeliner freckles. "It was almost as good as the real show!" Edgar mischievously exclaims.

In the year of the "I Fall to Pieces" routine, Edgar was co-producer of the Olio acts. "The other co-producer was Diane Bailey, whose two daughters were Summer Mummers mainstays," he explains. Working with a committee to write unabashedly silly skits was "very different for me," admits Edgar. "Having an engineering degree, I got kinda left out of fine art activities in college. In a way, I guess I'm kinda trying to make up for that." Though not the biggest role, Edgar's turn as a honky-tonk pianist was at least more memorable than his acting debut. "I was in the senior play in high school," Edgar recounts in a bright, slightly self-deprecating tone. "I had one line: 'Where do you want these, ma'am?' It was a western. Ladies were coming off of a stagecoach and checking into a hotel. I carried their luggage."

Edgar, incorrigibly left-brained, appreciates Mummers partly as a study in psychology. "Mummers is unique because it's a product of the audiences. Over the years, you learn what the audience likes and doesn't like." Thus, the melodrama conforms and re-conforms to the audience's fluctuating tastes. There was a similar liquidity to be found in Mummers' seating at the former American Legion Hall. Edgar observes, "It was also interesting to watch, as the production went on, how people tended to want to move closer and closer to the stage. The tables and chairs migrated closer to the stage until very few were remaining at the back. It was like the seating had a life of its own."

It's not just Summer Mummers that changes from year to year; it's the theatre, too. Edgar reflects, "Thinking back to what MCT was like when my wife and I came here in

December of 1957, the difference is night and day, particularly the quality of the cast. In the old days, typically, the leads would be really good and the rest of the cast weak. Today, typically, the entire cast top-to-bottom is extraordinary."Another aspect of the Midland Community Theatre that's kept changing with the times is its venue. MCT's first venue was a humble Quonset hut. In 1958, MCT migrated to its second home, "a plain-vanilla facility quite adequate for its time," as Edgar recalls. In 1978, the organization built a more architecturally remarkable theatre on Wadley Street. With visible pride, Edgar says, "The new one is state-of-the-art. It's been very important in attracting theatre-goers and staff."

Edgar doesn't restrict his theatre-going to Mummers productions. On the contrary, "I try to see as many productions as I can for variety." But, the oilman admits, he does have a preference: "I like the big spectacular musicals, *My Fair Lady*, *The Music Man*. And I like, of course, Neil Simon's comedies very much." When asked if he'll ever grace the stage again, Edgar is dubious. "Not unless I had a dynamite [Olio] act I'd want to do."

It hardly matters whether Edgar will appear on stage again because, charming as it is to watch him shed his engineer's shyness, his real contribution to MCT happens behind the scenes. Edgar's involvement with MCT began in 1976 when he was invited by an exiting board member to take his place. At the time, the theatre had only one board: a board of governors responsible for the theatre's day-to-day operations.

"The oil field workforce has always been young. By the time you're forty-five, you may not want—or be able—to do that kind of hard physical work anymore." - GIANT Dr. Diana Davids Hinton

Photo courtesy of Hendershot Photography

The petroleum engineer recalls his naive acceptance, "I thought it would be fun. My wife and I had gone to a number of productions, so I thought, 'Well, this'll be a fun way to learn how the theatre operates and pay back the community.'"

Unfortunately, Edgar's predecessor failed to warn his replacement of the board's impending annual meeting. When Edgar showed up at his first board meeting a few weeks later, he learned that not only had he missed the yearly powwow, but he'd also been elected Treasurer in his absence. A fairly unflappable man, Edgar says he "just kinda shrugged and thought, 'How hard it could be?'" "Well," he continues wryly, "I found out how hard it could be very quickly." First of all, he learned that MCT wanted a new building and was gearing up for a massive fundraising campaign. Edgar thought confidently, "Ok, I can handle that." Then the Secretary handed him the Treasurer's report, which bore a discouraging balance of just eighty-seven dollars.

"When the lights come up...you'll be knee-deep in popcorn."

The new building campaign wasn't the only challenge facing the accidental treasurer; Edgar also had to sort out the fiscal year's budget. The items were so numerous and complex that "it looked to me like the federal budget." But, he concedes, it turned out to be a great exercise. "As I went through line by line, I gained a very quick insight into how the theatre worked. To understand any organization, you really need to be familiar with the financials."

Eventually, enough funds were raised for the new building. The board, impressed by Edgar's cool management during a financially challenging year, urged him on to a second term as Treasurer, then two terms as President. In the early 80s, MCT established an endowment fund and a Board of Trustees to oversee it. Edgar is one of only three charter members still serving as an MCT Trustee.

Though his community involvement with MCT and other nonprofits keeps Edgar quite busy, the petroleum engineer still makes time for attending Summer Mummers. A drive down the theatre's alley won't yield the same eye-popping sights as the 70s, but out-of-towners can still be astonished. To his guests, Edgar always issues this caveat: "At the end of the show, when the lights come up, it's going to be the most disgusting sight you've ever seen. You'll be knee-deep in popcorn." And on that point, Edgar grins, "they're never disappointed. They always agree that I warned them appropriately."

prairie dunes

Joe Gifford enjoys visiting the Monahans Sandhills, where the terrain calls to mind a couple of adventure-filled years spent in the Algerian Sahara.

Joe Gifford

GIANT RISK

Joe Gifford's first clue that his foreign assignment would be life-endangering came when he saw his one-and-a-half-year-old daughter crawling unconcernedly along the narrow ledge outside their hotel suite. The toddler Houdini had crept out of a floor-to-ceiling French window and was now admiring Paris from a bird's-eye view.

Thinking quickly, Gifford's wife snatched up a box of cookies and placed it temptingly just inside the window. After a few excruciating seconds, the little girl was back inside devouring the sugary bait. Gifford, his wife, their six-week-old son, three-year-old daughter, and one-and-a-half-year-old daredevil were in France for a two-week orientation. Afterwards, Sinclair Mediterranean Petroleum Company moved its Chief Geologist and his young family to Algiers, right into the maw of the Algerian War.

The Algerian War was a colonial war waged between Algerian nationalists and French colonialists. Prior to its nineteenth-century colonization by the French, Algeria had enjoyed three centuries of autonomy as a province of the Ottoman Empire. When Joe Gifford arrived in Algiers in 1960, Algerians had been struggling for six years to regain their sovereignty. The Algerians' originally pacific tactics had transformed into violent ones after French settlers quashed numerous diplomatic compromises and the radical FLN retaliated. The FLN, or National Liberation Front*, was a small faction of Algerians that practiced guerilla warfare. Their violent attacks were brutally countered by the French military, which resorted to gruesomely torturing and killing suspected FLN leaders. The city of Algiers, where Gifford was sent, had been severely wracked by such warfare from 1956 to 1957 and the city was still trembling.

Gifford figured he couldn't do better than the French police for neighbors.

Algiers was also overflowing with displaced people. Terrorist activity in Algeria's farmlands had forced rural folk into the capital city, creating an acute housing shortage. For three months, the Gifford family hunkered down in an Algiers hotel. Then a lovely villa, six miles outside of the city, became miraculously available. Perched on a steep cliff, it provided a gorgeous view of the multicolored Mediterranean Sea below. More importantly, the villa sat just across the street from the *gendarmerie*. Gifford figured he and his family couldn't do better than the French police for neighbors, so they moved in.

Gifford was linguistically unprepared for Algeria and relied on a young translator named Kebir. A handsome, taller-than-average Arab, Kebir was always well-groomed and well-spoken. His fluency in English, Arabic, and a Bedouin dialect soon proved invaluable to Gifford, as did the Arab's keen eye. One day, while chauffeuring Gifford from Algiers' airport to the center of town, Kebir spotted something unusual in the distance: a huge, agitated crowd of villagers. Sensing danger, Kebir pulled off the main highway and took a back-road path to Algiers, bypassing the frenzied village. Later, Gifford learned the cause of the hubbub: the locals had beheaded four Frenchmen that day.

CAREER HIGHLIGHTS

1952 Graduates with BA in geology from University of Nebraska

1952-1954 Serves in the U.S. Army

1954-1955 Attends grad school at the University of Nebraska under Sinclair Fellowship

1955 Goes to work for Sinclair

1960-1961 Sinclair's Chief Geologist in Algeria

1962-1964 Sinclair's Chief Geologist in Paris

1964-1966 Sinclair's District Manager of the Permian Basin

1966 Leaves Sinclair; Joins Bill Roden as an independent oilman

1966 Gifford's first well as an independent, the Roden Oil Co. #1 Wolf Unit in Winkler County, erupts into one of the biggest blowouts in Texas, requiring Red Adair and forty-eight days to extinguish

1966 Gifford sells his interests in #1 Wolf Unit to become a multimillionaire overnight

1975 Forms GMW Corporation

1978 GMW Corp. boasts five twenty-thousand-feet wells running at one time, more than any other U.S. company at the time

1982 Forms TriTex Petroleum Company

1988 Ceases operating wells

2002 Enters semi-retirement

2008 Gifford still relishes oil exploration and participates in many deals

Even though Gifford was an American, his otherness would have made him an appealing target. Kebir's shrewd circumnavigation most likely saved Gifford's life.

Algeria above-ground was deadly dangerous to foreigners, but what lay below-ground made America-based Sinclair Oil willing to take the risk. It had recently, with Gifford's assistance, discovered a billion-barrel oilfield in the middle of the Sahara Desert and was determined to develop the site. Sinclair accompanied their first oil well with a water well, the second task not being nearly as difficult as one might think. Hidden under the mercilessly dry surface of the Algerian Sahara is a giant Cretaceous aquifer: a sandy, water-bearing geological layer from which free-flowing artesian wells can be sprung. Sinclair's first Saharan oil well turned out to be a dry hole, but its first water well was surprisingly successful. One morning, Gifford gazed out his cubicle's window and beheld a camel herd placidly watering at the well. It appeared that the oil company had unknowingly drilled on a Bedouin caravan route. The nomadic people and their beasts of burden were delighted with the new water source. Shortly thereafter, the Bedouin tribe's chief came to Gifford's office and asked if he would be so kind as to get government permission to leave the well intact after Sinclair moved on. And, in anticipated gratitude, the chief invited Gifford to a feast the next morning.

The Bedouins lived in large tents shaped much like American camping tents, but with slightly rounded corners. Goat hides, hair facing out, were stretched like tarpaulins over the tent supports. Gifford asked his companion Kebir why the Bedouins left the goats' coarse black hair on the hides: Wouldn't their dark color absorb an unbearable amount of the Saharan sun? Kebir replied that no, the tents were actually quite cool thanks to those dark skins. Gifford, unsure of the physics behind such an assertion, shrugged and entered the chief's tent. The geologist's work-booted feet sunk unsuspectingly into sumptuous, handwoven rugs. The entire sandy floor was covered with them, except for a small corner where chickens were quarantined. Gifford breathed in and noted that, despite the indoor fowl, the air was oddly odorless. Then he noticed the large, gauzy curtain bisecting the tent lengthwise. Gifford thought he heard some quiet movements and murmurs on the other side, but he couldn't see anyone.

Photo courtesy of Yellow Wood Photography

After cordial greetings were exchanged, his Bedouin host proudly served tea. More surprising than the tea's syrupy sweetness was its dainty presentation in, of all things, porcelain cups. However, the subsequent courses bore no such hints of westernization. The Bedouins had prepared a goat *mechoui* and presented Gifford with a bowl of its most coveted part—the eyeballs. The white, gooey orbs stared up at the guest of honor.

Gifford, his stomach already churning, had to think fast. "Oh, thank you. I would be honored," Gifford smoothly responded through the medium of Kebir, "but I can't take them in good conscience because I am not the one with power." Gifford gestured to his right-hand man, "You see, Kebir, here, is the rightful recipient. It is he who will present your water-well case to the government."

It was a boldfaced lie, but a kind one. Whereas Gifford feared he'd vomit after eating those sticky spheres, he knew Kebir would relish the dish. The ruse worked. The chief passed the bowl of honor to a grateful Kebir, and Gifford kept his lunch down.

As the unlikely trio dined, they engaged in small talk:
The Bedouin inquired, "Where do you come from?"
"I come from the United States," Gifford answered.
"Where is that?"
"It's across the ocean."
"Do you [the United States] have an army?"
"Yes, a pretty large army."
"Do you have a camel corps?"
"No."
"Well, it must not be a very powerful army, then," the Bedouin concluded smugly.
Gifford, wanting to be a good guest, decided not to disillusion his host.

Now that politics were out of the way, the conversation shifted to family matters. The Bedouin inquired if Gifford had any children. "Yes," replied the proud father and proffered a photograph. The chief inspected the glossy image interestedly and asked, "May I show my wife?" "Sure," said Gifford. He watched curiously as his host slipped his dark-skinned hand through a slit in the gauzy curtain and gave the photo to an invisible recipient. From behind the partition rose a soft, feminine gasp of surprise, followed by giggling. It was then apparent that the tribe's women were occupying the unseen half of the tent. It was also apparent that the women had never seen a white-skinned, yellow-haired child before, much less three of them. After several minutes of study, the photo was passed back

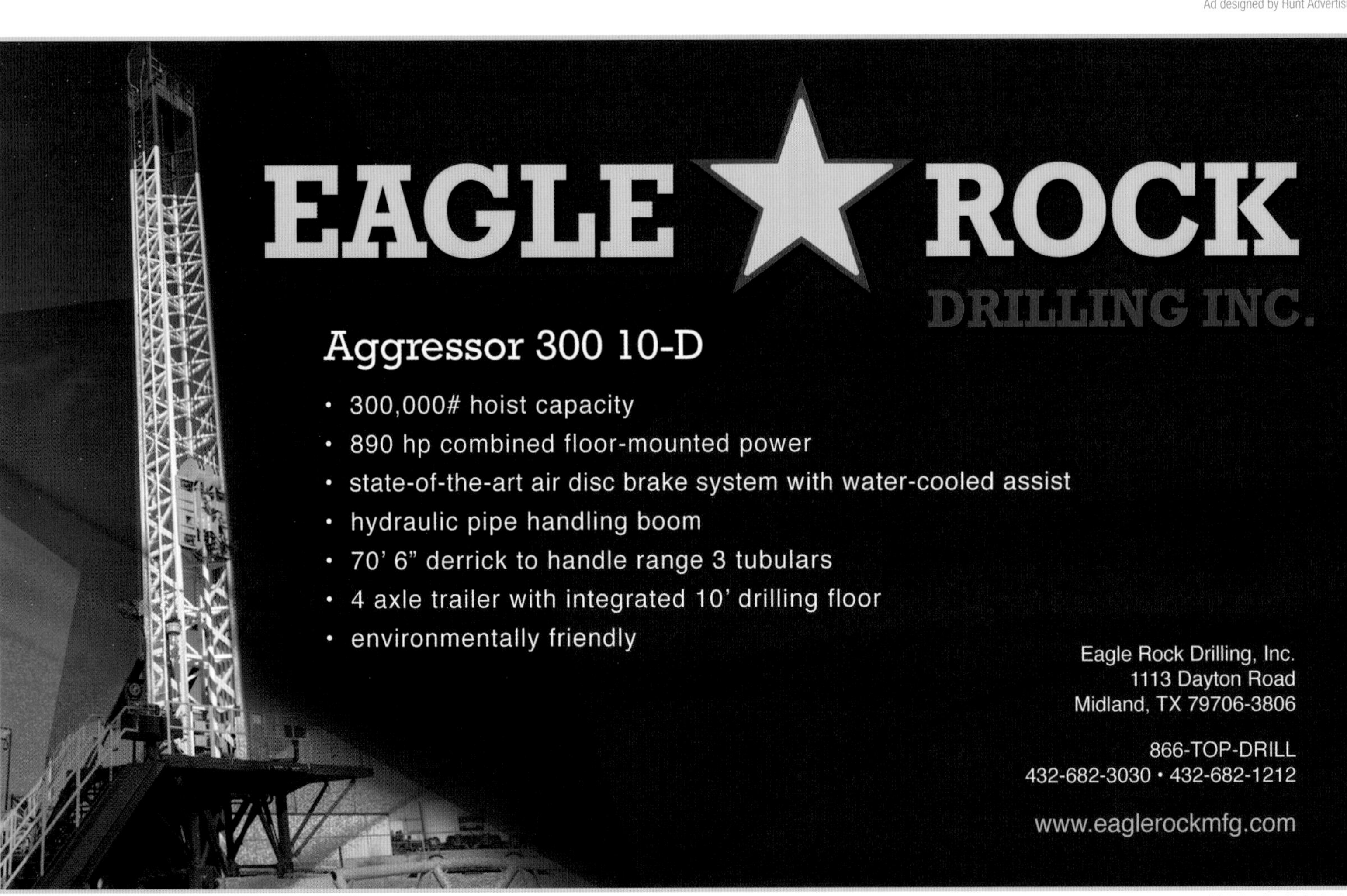

EAGLE ROCK
DRILLING INC.
Aggressor 300 10-D
• 300,000# hoist capacity
• 890 hp combined floor-mounted power
• state-of-the-art air disc brake system with water-cooled assist
• hydraulic pipe handling boom
• 70' 6" derrick to handle range 3 tubulars
• 4 axle trailer with integrated 10' drilling floor
• environmentally friendly
Eagle Rock Drilling, Inc.
1113 Dayton Road
Midland, TX 79706-3806
866-TOP-DRILL
432-682-3030 • 432-682-1212
www.eaglerockmfg.com

through the curtain and returned to Gifford. When Kebir and Gifford finally made their gracious exit, they did so with full bellies and a feeling of human solidarity.

Whereas the Bedouins made Gifford feel welcome, the Fellagha, a terrorist rebel group, did just the opposite. Even ensconced in their picturesque country villa, Gifford and his family were not safe. Bullets pinged off their red-tiled roof when the Fellagha charged down from the nearby mountains and ambushed the *gendarmerie*. That time, Gifford and his family waited out the crisis in the villa's underground boathouse. But when a Spanish family two-doors-down was mercilessly beheaded, baby included, for their suspected association with the French secret police, Gifford knew his family had to leave immediately. He sent his wife and children to Mallorca and moved himself into an Algiers apartment.

Bullets pinged off their red-tiled roof

To counter the Fellagha, French military leaders had joined with Algerian settlers to form a secret army organization (OAS). The Fellagha were creating terror however they could, lobbing bombs into outdoor cafes and grenades into school buses. The Fellagha were also living up to their name, "cutting off" communication by murdering postmen. The OAS countered with *plastiques* (plastic bombs), which shredded Arab businesses and cast the sky an ominous, unnatural blue. But, despite this life-threatening chaos, Gifford and his colleagues soldiered on with their Sinclair work.

One December night in 1961, Gifford was blown from his bed by a bomb that shattered his apartment's windows and razed to the ground a nearby building. For Gifford and his equally ruffled manager, this more-than-rude awakening was the last straw. Early the next morning they sent a Telex to Sinclair's headquarters in New York saying they were done living in a war zone and would henceforth control the Sahara's subsurface remotely.

By the time Algeria won its independence in 1962, Gifford and his family were safely settled back in Paris. To show for his trials, Gifford had little more than a few ancient relics he had discovered among the Saharan sands: ostrich eggs, arrowheads, wooden toys and other anthropological detritus unearthed by the dune-shifting desert wind. Internally, however, Gifford came away with something quite valuable: a well-developed tolerance for crises. He'd apply this talent just a few years later to the blowout of his first independent oil well.

* *The acronym FLN derives from the group's French name:* Front de libération nationale.

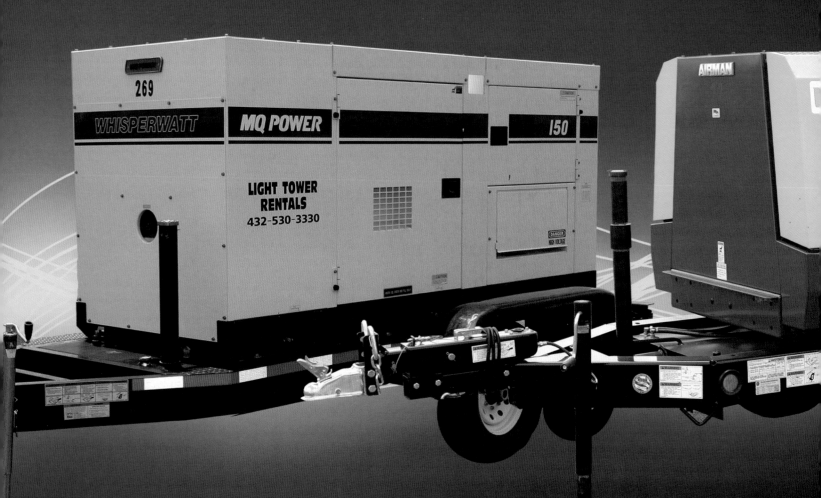

LIGHT TOWER
RENTAL PRODUCTS:
Trailer Houses • Light Towers
Generators • Frac Tanks
Trash Trailers • Acid Tanks
Flow Back Tanks
Air Compressors
Fresh Water Systems
LIGHT TOWER
RENTALS
432-530-3330
AIRMAN
PDS185S
LTR
Allmand
MAXI-LITE 895
LIGHT TOWER
RENTALS
432-530-3330
SHO
Ad designed by Hunt Advertising

Standing atop one of Midland's tallest buildings, Jim Henry admits, "I'm really a little afraid of heights, not too much, but some." Considering Henry literally jumps at the chance for adventure, you'd never know he has this touch of acrophobia.

Jim Henry

GIANT DARING

Jim Henry, a slender young man about fifteen years old, on summer retreat with the First Baptist Church of Oklahoma City, cooled himself in the blue-green pool beneath Turner Falls. Oklahoma's oldest park, Turner Falls is the picturesque point where springs from the Arbuckle Mountains cascade down a seventy-seven-foot cliff and collect in a natural swimming pool.

The cliff's jagged edge cleaves the water into columns, leaving expanses of dry rock between the falls. It was one of these waterless gaps that attracted Henry's eye. He swam closer, scanning the rocky surface for footholds. He found some man-made footholds carved into the rock and began to climb. Higher and higher he went, urged on by the exhilarating rush and roar of the waterfalls. He didn't look down because, contrary to his actions, Henry was a little acrophobic. Soon, the crown of his head was higher than the cliff's top. Henry enthusiastically swung his right leg onto the summit before noticing how dangerously slick the mossy rock looked. Henry panicked. "If I try to stand on this moss," he thought, "I'll surely slip and die." Henry glanced down and the sight was worse than expected. Other adventurers had clambered up behind him, blocking his escape route. Henry recalls, "I first panicked. Then, all of a sudden, a tremendous calm came over me and I thought, "if I'm going to die, I'm going to die and the Lord'll take care of me." He took a breath and placed his right foot on the moss. To his great surprise, the moss wasn't slippery at all and his step placed him safely on the cliff's top, just a short distance from the highway.

Higher and higher he went, urged on by the exhilarating roar of the waterfalls.

A few years later, Henry had another memorable scare. It was 1963 and Henry, now in his 20s, was enthusiastically participating in the Hospital Follies. Humble Oil had transferred him to Midland, Texas, two years earlier to progress his oil career. The Hospital Follies, a now-defunct fundraiser for the local hospital, gave amateurs like Henry the chance to perform for an audience of several hundred. Passionate about charity and theatre, Henry was easily sold on the idea. He didn't experience a hint of stage fright until his tux went missing a few minutes before his act. He scrambled about backstage, upending props and raking through costume racks, but to no avail. His tuxedo had vanished. There was no choice but to beg a costume off a fellow performer. Minutes later, as he fidgeted with the cuffs of his borrowed suit, Henry heard something that made his stomach sink deeper. There, performing the act just before his own, was the talented Jane Parker. Henry recalls with admiration, "She was singing this torch song and doing a fabulous job of it!" Listening to her magnificent voice, the young oilman wished he could disappear as inexplicably as his tux. Memorization had never been Henry's strong suit and Parker's song was working on his mind like an eclipse. By her last sonorous note, Henry had forgotten every line of his own song. "You're on," directed the stage manager. Henry wasn't a professional, but he had spent enough time in community theatre to know a cardinal rule of acting: "If you can't do something, fake it, but do it with all your energy." Accordingly, the young man ran headlong onto stage, grinning ear to ear. Exuberantly snapping up the

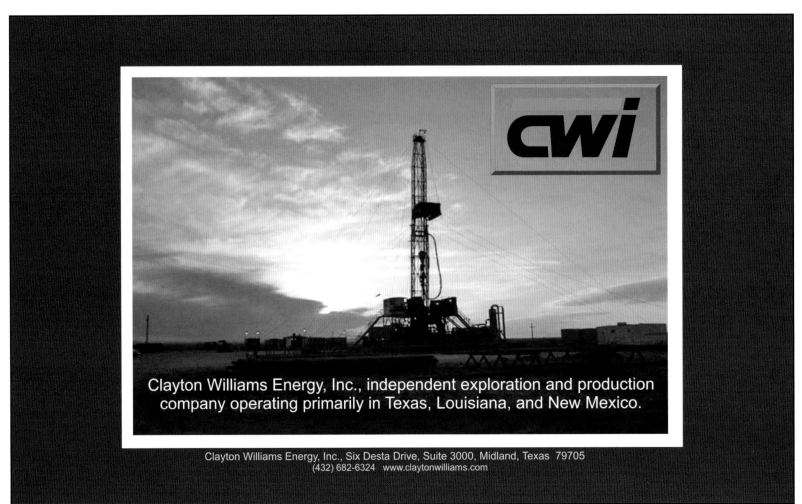

CAREER HIGHLIGHTS

1958 Graduates from University of Oklahoma with Master's in petroleum engineering; enters U.S. Air Force as a Lieutenant

1960 Works for Humble Oil & Refining Co. in Houston, TX

1961 Moves to Midland, TX

1964 Works for Skelly Oil Co. in Tulsa, OK

Jan 1969 Leaves Skelly for Solar Oil Co. in Midland

Nov 1969 Leaves Solar; Starts H & L Consultants

1971 Becomes oil operator dba Henry & Landenberger Inc.; turns first big deal in Spraberry trend called the 6-6-3 project

1977 Bob Landenberger retires; company becomes Henry Petroleum

1988 ARCO Petroleum hands over operations at Shafter Lake to Henry Petroleum

1998 Dennis Johnson becomes President of Henry Petroleum and Henry becomes CEO, leaving Henry more time to work in civic affairs: United Way, Casa de Amigos, Permian Basin Petroleum Association and others

2004 Henry Petroleum accumulates large acreage position in Wolfberry trend (Wolfcamp + Spraberry), two-thirds of acreage proves good

2007 Johnson leaves Henry Petroleum and Ronnie Scott becomes President

2008 Henry estimates at least five more years of drilling in Wolfberry acreage using eight rigs

Jul 2008 Henry sells to Concho Resources and starts over as Henry Resources

microphone, Henry launched into song. The words and melody miraculously came back to him. And, because the piece had a fast tempo, it did not require from him as much skill as Jane Parker had exhibited. During the second verse, the chorus came on stage and helped Jim finish the song. The audience clapped appreciatively and Henry strode offstage, happy that he had performed well.

For a few years after the appropriately named Follies, Henry's life was free from jeopardy. In 1964 he married Paula Hargrove, whom he still lovingly calls "the most important person in my life." In late 1964, Jim accepted a job with Skelly Oil in Tulsa, Oklahoma where his daughters, Jamie and Beverly, were born. Later, a third child, David, was born. By 1969, Henry was back in Midland under the employ of Solar Oil, which was struggling. With Solar's demise imminent, Henry had a momentous decision to make. First, he conferred with his wife, "Paula, we can either start our own company or I can go back to work for a major oil company." A calculated risk-taker just like her husband, Paula reasoned, "Let's try it. If it doesn't work out, you can always go back to a major oil company." Henry agreed. For a business partner, he chose Bob Landenberger. The two had worked together for Skelly Oil: Henry as chief engineer, Landenberger as chief geologist. Skill-wise they were set, but capital-wise they were sorely lacking. At the time, Henry and his wife had one- and three-year-old children, no savings, and only their home for equity. Landenberger was even less financially equipped with six kids and no savings. They built H&L Consultants with sweat-equity. Henry recounts proudly, "We never missed a paycheck in my whole career. We came close a year after starting, but everything worked out fine."

Henry's oil career flourished enough over the next four decades to keep him out of trouble. The next chance to be daring didn't present itself until 2006, when he and Paula sojourned in New Zealand. The Henrys were gazing out the windows of their tour vehicle when they noticed the verdant foliage wasn't brushing by as quickly. Their guide was softly applying the brake as they neared a people-filled bridge. "We can stop here if you want," the driver offered. They were, he explained, at Queenstown's Kawarau Bridge, the world's first commercial bungee jumping site. Since 1988, tens of thousands

VIKING
RIG 1

of adventure-seekers had plunged forty-three meters down into the turquoise waters below. His three kids had all bungee jumped and lived to tell the tale—why couldn't he? He posed this seemingly logical question to his wife, who found it far less compelling. "You are not! You will hurt your back," Paula retorted. As Henry neared the bridge, his confidence began to wane. Secretly, he hoped there'd be a long line so he'd only have to show the intention of jumping.

As luck would have it, there was not a long line. The oilman signed the release form and submitted to the bungee crew. Nervous as he was, he still had enough of his engineer's bearing to scrutinize their preparations. He felt the strength of the body harness and the firmness of the bungee hook. "That bungee cord was not coming off and I was glad about that," remembers Henry. A thickly accented instructor led him to the jumping platform, urging, "Git yur toes to the idge, now." Henry, his ankles tethered together, obediently tottered forward. One hand still clinging to the bridge, Henry hatched a plan. Like the Hospital Follies years before, he was going to give the moment his all. He was going to act fearless, even if he didn't really feel fearless. He released his grip on the bridge. He raised his arms in front of him, curling his hands into interlocked fists that would break the water before it could break him. "On 'Three,' " Henry recounts, "I jumped as hard as I could. I pushed off that platform with all my might." Falling through the air was exhilarating, but Henry didn't have time to enjoy it. It only lasted three seconds.

"I believe life, to the end, has got to be a daring adventure."

As is typical with risky activities, the dive didn't go exactly as planned. Henry had selected the "water touch option" in which only his arms and the top of his head were to get wet. But an apparent miscalculation resulted in Henry being dunked tip to toe. This surprise submersion didn't faze Henry, though. "I went in like a professional—didn't hardly make a splash," Henry says proudly, then concedes that his textbook diver's form *was* aided by the bungee cord holding his ankles fast together. Grinning at the memory of the 141-foot plunge, he enthuses, "It is a tremendous experience to free fall—I would like to go skydiving."

Henry loves to push himself to the edge, whether it's the edge of exhaustion when he's exercising, the edge of a bridge when he's vacationing, or the edge of technology when he's trying to make a low-return oil well profitable. For role models, he turns to historical figures who've exhibited the same penchant for self-challenge. Henry says feelingly, "I believe in Helen Keller." Quoting Keller, the businessman intones, "*Security is mostly a superstition. It does not exist in nature. Life is either a daring adventure or nothing.*" Henry beams, "I love that saying and I believe life, to the end, has got to be a daring adventure."

Carbon dioxide, when pumped deep into oil fields, decreases crude's viscosity and facilitates recovery. Here, the release of carbon dioxide creates a dense fog.

Photo courtesy of Hendershot Photography

Dr. Diana Davids Hinton fleshes out her newest book, *Oil in Texas,* on her preferred medium—legal pads. Not until she has handwritten the final draft, footnotes and all, will she commit her words to type.

Dr. Diana Davids Hinton

GIANT HISTORIAN

Mrs. X sneered through the peephole at the Yankee on her doorstep. What was this young woman with the Yale doctorate up to if not muckraking? Grudgingly the septuagenarian opened the door. The ingénue readjusted the tape recorder in the crook of her arm, proffered her hand and said, "Hi, Mrs. X. I'm Diana Olien. It's a pleasure to meet you."

Mrs. X limply took her hand and made a facial expression that could be interpreted as either a smile or a grimace, depending on one's optimism. "Tell me again what this book is about," prompted the hostess as she led Diana through the large, bric-a-brac-laden rooms. Diana dutifully recounted how she and her husband, Roger—a professor at UTPB—were endeavoring to debunk popular oil-boom myths by writing about previous booms. Their study would focus on five West Texas towns: Midland, Odessa, Snyder, McCamey, and Wink. Many Snyder residents had suggested that Mrs. X could provide an invaluable account of the 1948-1951 boom in Scurry County. Mrs. X responded with another smile/grimace.

The two women reached a heavily-decorated dining room and Mrs. X gestured for Diana to sit. Setting her tape recorder on the table, Diana debated. There were batteries in her recorder, but what if they died in the middle of the interview and she missed some commentary while reloading? No. Better to play it safe, she decided. She uncoiled the thick black cord and plugged it into a nearby wall socket. Good thing I didn't bring Nina along to this one, thought Diana. Though she's a well-behaved little scout, she'd probably ask Mrs. X if she had any toys she could play with. Diana could just imagine the fear that would flash in Mrs. X's eyes when she looked down at Nina and pictured those three-year-old fists crushing all her precious figurines. Diana stifled a chuckle and checked that a new tape was loaded in the recorder.

Mrs. X rose from her seat, walked over to a wall switch and flipped it off.

The writer looked up from her equipment to find Mrs. X appraising her coolly from the opposite chair. Discomfited, Diana hastily finished her preparations, pressed the record button, and began, "Mrs. X, what year did you move to Snyder?" Before answering, Mrs. X rose from her seat, walked over to a wall switch and flipped it off. This action seemed reasonable to Diana; after all, the room was lit well enough from the window and they didn't really need the fan. Mrs. X returned to her seat and answered the question without elaboration. She answered each subsequent question with similar taciturnity—no personal commentary, just the facts. Even worse, Mrs. X fired questions back: Why was Diana so interested in the Scurry County boom? Who would be reading this book she was writing? Who else had she and her husband interviewed? Diana, fighting back frustration, reminded herself that West Texans had every right to be wary of writers. After all, it was the mainstream media's misrepresentation of this area that she was seeking to redress.

Four hours later, Diana dropped wearily onto her motel bed with her writer's paraphernalia. Sighing, she held down rewind for a minute, then pressed play on her recorder to

Ad designed by Hunt Advertising.

Ad designed by Hunt Advertising.

CAREER HIGHLIGHTS

1964 Graduates with High Honors and Phi Beta Kappa from Swarthmore College, BA in history, minors in fine arts and philosophy

1966 Earns Master of Arts in history from Yale University

1967 Earns Master of Philosophy in history from Yale University

1969 Graduates with PhD in history from Yale University

1969-1973 Assistant Professor of History, Southern Methodist University, Dallas, TX

1982 *Oil Booms: Social Change in Five Texas Towns* published. Co-author: Roger M. Olien

1983 *Morpeth: A Victorian Public Career* published.

1984 *Wildcatters: Texas Independent Oilmen* published. Co-author: Roger M. Olien

1986 *Life in the Oil Fields* published. Co-author: Roger M. Olien

1984, 2001-2003 Part-time Instructor in History, Midland College, Midland, TX

1986-1989 Adjunct Instructor in History, University of Texas of the Permian Basin (UTPB), Odessa, TX

1989-2004 Senior Lecturer in History, UTPB

1990 *Easy Money: Oil Promoters and Investors in the Jazz Age* published. Co-author: Roger M. Olien.

1992 Named a Life Fellow of the Texas State Historical Association

1997 Presented with an Outstanding Teaching Award by UTPB's College of Arts and Sciences

2000 *Oil and Ideology: The Cultural Creation of the American Petroleum Industry* published. Co-author: Roger M. Olien.

2002 *Oil in Texas: The Gusher Age* published. Co-author: Roger M. Olien. The next year, the book garnered a citation by the San Antonio Conservation Society.

2004-Present Professor and J. Conrad Dunagan Chair of Regional and Business History, UTPB

2007 *Wildcatters: Texas Independent Oilmen* reissued, with a new introduction by Hinton. Co-author: Roger M. Olien.

2008 Hinton is co-writing *Oil in Texas: Maturity and Global Expansion* with longtime collaborator Roger M. Olien.

see if the day's interview sounded any better on tape than it did in her memory. Silence. Her heart quickening, Diana fast-forwarded a few minutes and played the tape again. There was just a lot of nothing. Horrified, Diana stared helplessly at the recorder. Then, a sickening memory surfaced: Mrs. X standing by the wall, nonchalantly flipping down a switch with her wrinkled index finger—cutting off power to the wall socket as well as the ceiling fixtures. It had been sabotage! That old woman had satisfied her own curiosity while making sure her visitor wouldn't come away with anything publishable.

Thirty years later, Diana (now Diana Davids Hinton) chuckles good-naturedly as she recalls getting duped, "The joke was on me on that one! After that I learned to monitor my equipment a lot more often." Fortunately, excepting the elderly saboteur, Hinton's interviewees for *Oil Booms* were very friendly and forthcoming. Remembers Hinton warmly, "One of the great things about that project was that we not only did a lot of work with local records, but also we got to visit with and interview a lot of people who had lived during the boom times—some had come out here in the '20s and had lived in tents. They were a lot of fun to visit with." She adds appreciatively, "For all of the works that I've done, the people here [in West Texas] have been wonderfully helpful."

Hinton attributes West Texans' receptivity partly to the region's rare breed of generosity. She observes, "I've lived other places, and West Texas really is a friendly sort of place. I have found that out here if people can possibly help you, they will." Furthermore,

Photo courtesy of Hendershot Photography

Hinton notes, West Texans in 1978 had a compelling motive for speaking to historians: *their* stories hadn't been sought out or recorded to the extent of other Texas regions. "I think people genuinely appreciated our being interested in their part of the past," says Hinton. Cocking her head thoughtfully, she adds, 'I think they wanted to share their history with us—maybe as much as we wanted to learn it from them."

Hinton is the J. Conrad Dunagan Chair of Regional and Business History at the University of Texas of the Permian Basin in Odessa, Texas. Her History of the American Petroleum Industry course, in particular, attracts students from every field of study. Hinton explains the class's popularity this way: "For a lot of people it's 'roots' time because their families or they [themselves] have been in the industry. That's a lot of fun." She continues, "I often tell students: History properly done tells you something about your own identity. And so, if someone is studying your history, that's like valuing your identity."

> "The phone doesn't ring when oil prices are low and you're an oil historian."

Not surprisingly, the amount that the nation at large values West Texas's identity fluctuates with the price of oil. The professor notes wryly, "Whenever oil prices are high, people call wanting to get interviews [from me]." For example, in the early days of the 1980s boom, Hinton recalls hoards of international television reporters descending upon the oil patch. There were Canadian reporters, Scandinavian reporters, NPR reporters—all giddily filling the air with electromagnetic waves and economic predictions. But, when the market plummeted a few years later, so did international interest. "The phone doesn't ring when [oil] prices are low [and] you're an oil historian," laughs Hinton.

Hinton is unconcerned by the feast-or-famine nature of her work. Like the successful oil men and women she writes about, the author has proven she has both the humor and the hardiness to be a part of this roller coaster industry. Besides, just because outsiders aren't always clamoring for information doesn't mean there's ever time to twiddle one's thumbs. The historian reports excitedly, "There's so much there that's left to be done—so many questions that can be investigated." Furthermore, even when people *aren't* asking questions about the oil industry, they *should* be. Showing a slight tinge of frustration, the professor says, "One of the things that's ironic about working on oil history is energy policy: We [America] keep on making the same mistakes again and again and again—the same type of unproductive things. They didn't work before; they won't work again." Then, quickly resuming her characteristic optimism, she concludes, "If the work I do can help people outside understand the industry better, then I will have felt I have accomplished something."

Eagle Strength & Power.
Eagle Manufacturing, Ltd., is committed to providing durable and dependable products to the world-wide oil and gas industry. We build our rigs strong and with the power to finish the job – time after time.
At Eagle, machining, mechanical and fabrication, as well as painting and product certification are all completed in-house. We build our own draw works, derricks and chassis. And by not relying on off-site services, we control our workmanship, minimize product cost, and deliver optimum quality and satisfaction to our customers–on time- every time.
At Eagle, our goal is to continually meet or exceed our customers' expectations. By adhering to API and ISO standards, we are able to consistently perform at this level and deliver top quality equipment that will stand – the test of time.
Now is the time–Call or visit our website:
Eagle Manufacturing, Ltd.
13600 W. I-20 East
Odessa, Texas USA
432-561-7000 Ph
432-561-7010 FAX
www.eaglerigusa.com
EAGLE
MANUFACTURING
• Rig Models - 300 series- 650 series
• Masts & Derricks - From 96 ft. - 225,000 lbs. up to 118 ft. - 450,000 lbs.
EAGLE manufactures our rig parts in Texas, USA, and offers field services on any model.
API LICENSED • ISO CERTIFIED
No. 4F-0170

When she began researching the Texas oil industry, Hinton was delighted to find a quality that much nineteenth-century British scholarship lacked: novelty. She describes this almost-magical discovery as "going to the beach early in the morning when the tide has gone in and out and there are no footprints on the beach and you can be the first one." Or, in the case of Diana Hinton and Roger Olien, among the first. Over the past thirty years, the two have pumped from this untrodden ground enough content to fill six books, as well as countless essays, articles and scholarly papers. Hinton explains, "My former husband and I could do most books fairly quickly. The book that took the longest to do was called *Oil and Ideology—that* took us nearly ten years!" Still collaborators today, Hinton and Olien are in the process of penning their seventh book together. Plus, Hinton's got several solo works in mind, including her magnum opus. "I want to do one volume by myself: a reader-friendly history of the American petroleum industry," confides Hinton. "The last one of its kind came out in the '60s and has a tremendous amount of complicated details the average reader wouldn't want to read." She smiles, envisioning her history for the masses, then says modestly, "If I have a dream, I guess that's it."

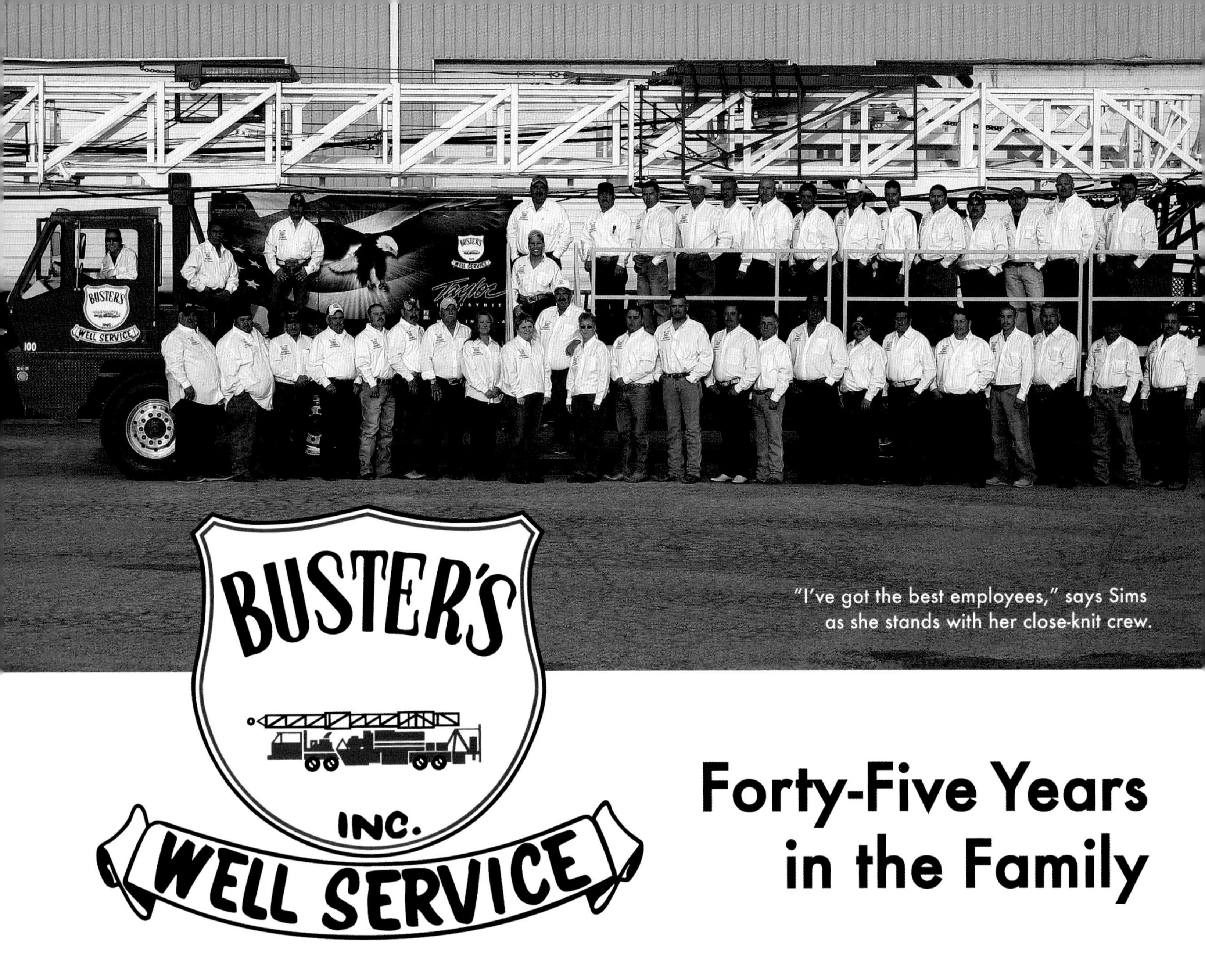

"I've got the best employees," says Sims as she stands with her close-knit crew.

Forty-Five Years in the Family

On June 19, 2008, Buster's Well Service celebrated its 45th anniversary. Had its founder Buster Crabtree been alive to enjoy it, he would've bestowed upon granddaughter Angie Sims a rare pat on the back. Thank you for keeping my legacy alive—for pulling my company back from the brink of destruction—for loving it and its workers as much as I did—that's what his hand on her shoulder blades would've said for this man of few words.

Alex "Buster" Crabtree moved from Albany to Kermit, Texas, with his wife, Nell, in 1938. He applied for work with his brother-in-law's employer, Sid Richardson, and also with J.P. "Bum" Gibbons's well service company. Fatefully, Bum called him first. Buster began as a rig hand. Over the next twenty-five years he advanced to an operator and then a pusher. The energy and integrity with which Buster applied himself did not go unnoticed by his boss, who made him a top hand.

In 1963, Buster's employer retired. A generous man, Bum gave his top hands the opportunity to purchase the yards and equipment before he put them up for public sale. Buster and a few other men took advantage of the offer, carving the assets into the beginnings of several service companies. As of 2006, only three of these spin-offs were still in operation. And, today, Buster's is one of only two extant companies that stemmed directly from Bum.

Buster's Well Service, Inc. • P.O. Box 1119 • Kermit, Texas 79745

Buster, with his trustworthiness and dependability, engendered so much

Buster Crabtree set about building a successful family business. For Buster, "family business" signified two things: one, a business to be passed down to his son and his son's sons and so on; and two, a business whose employees had the loyalty of a family. Buster, with his trustworthiness and dependability, soon engendered so much respect in his workers that, as Angie puts it, "they would have fought a circular saw for him." The entire town of Kermit felt much the same way and Buster's line of credit was good wherever he went.

Applying natural business acumen, Buster steadily grew his company over the next three decades. In the mid-1980s when the bust crippled many neighboring businesses, Buster's Well Service weathered the storm and kept its workforce intact. Without a doubt, Buster had no problem surviving external crises. The only thing that ultimately proved too strong an adversary for him was cancer. In 1997, after thirty-four years helming his own business, Buster passed away. His well service went to his only son.

Unfortunately, Buster's son quickly proved unfit for business ownership. After several disastrous years of his mismanagement, Buster's Well Service and its workers' morale were in shambles. Angie Sims, finally of age to take control of her inherited shares, felt obliged to step in and right her uncle's wrongs. Using what she calls "simple household economics," Angie got Buster's books back on track. She even put her personal credit on the line to help pay off some of the debts her uncle had amassed.

Angie worked equally hard on restoring the trust of Buster's workers, suppliers, and clients. To them, she admitted her newness to the well-servicing industry and invited their tutelage. She also gained their respect by showing she wasn't above grunt work—one time scaling a rig and cleaning it top to bottom single-handedly.

By 2007, Kermit's Chamber of Commerce had taken note of Buster's Well Service's prodigious transformation and named it Business of the Year. Today, the company has nearly fifty employees, any of whom, Angie ventures, "would fight a circular saw for me, just like they would've for Grandpa."

1963, Pole rig converted to a double-triple

Rig from the early 1970s

In 2008, Buster's Well Service bought a new rig and dedicated it to Grandpa Buster, giving it his radio call number of 100.

ph 432.586.2533 • fax 432.586.9636 • bws1963@cebridge.net

respect in his workers that "they would have fought a circular saw for him."

Harvey Page sinks a putt while his wife, Peggy, cheers him on. Though he looks quite professional on the Odessa Country Club's greens, the Ref-Chem Chairman and CEO is quick to admit, "I'm a bogey golfer. My philosophy is: I know if I'm shooting under 90, I'm playing too much golf; if I'm over 90, I'm working too hard." Page has been balancing work and play since age ten.

Harvey Page

GIANT WORK ETHIC

It appeared the entire population of Oakley, Kansas had come out to celebrate harvest's end. So many bodies in such a tight space—it was hard to keep track of them all. Perched on his lifeguard post, Harvey Page took a rough count of the bobbing heads and came up with close to a hundred.

Good thing I shelled out the extra bucks for two more guards today, thought Page, absentmindedly scratching the sun-bleached hair on his arm. Just then, a glistening patch of water caught Page's eye—a kid had been there a second ago—he was sure of it. Blowing his whistle in a vain attempt to disperse the crowd, Page dove into the pool. He shoved through the slippery jungle of elbows and knees, keeping his eye on the submerged boy. Ducking beneath the water, he caught hold of the drowning child's torso and hauled him to the surface. A few seconds later, he was helping the boy cough up water onto the hot cement. Not long afterwards, another lifeguard would provide similar assistance to a farmhand who hadn't let inexperience dissuade him from the deep end. After the third save, Page and his exasperated crew were beginning to wonder, Who else was down there? Page decided to institute a new rule on the spot: everybody out of the pool, every hour, so the guards could reassure themselves that no one was trapped below.

He caught hold of the drowning child's torso and hauled him to the surface.

By the time the crowd dispersed, water-logged and ready for their Fourth of July dinners, Page and his staff were exhausted. Page had pulled four people out of the water that day, which, added to the other guards' saves, made a total of six. Six life-endangering accidents, a few of which had even required CPR—Page shook his head—thank goodness lifeguarding wasn't always like this. Most days his pool job consisted of pumping chlorine gas, cleaning the pool and playing babysitter to a bunch of farm kids. That lot didn't give him much trouble because even the littlest ones knew better than to get banned from the only hangout in town. Plus, their parents would whoop them into next year if their bad behavior lost what amounted to three months of free childcare!

That day, Page's most memorable Fourth of July, occurred in 1960, just before his senior year at Kansas State. He had begun working at Oakley's municipal pool as a seventh grader, helping his cousin and her husband run the newly built facility. Since then, Page had mastered pool maintenance and earned his lifeguard and water safety instructor certifications. Now, the city paid him a thousand dollars a month to manage the pool himself. From that amount, he had to pay his staff—a cleaning boy, concession help and some extra lifeguards for the weekends—but that still left Page with four-hundred dollars a month. Plus, he made additional money teaching water safety lessons and selling concessions. Considering gasoline only cost around a quarter a gallon at the time, Page's pool job paid quite well.

CAREER HIGHLIGHTS

1961 Graduates from Kansas State College (now University) with a degree in civil engineering; hired by Phillips Petroleum and moves to Odessa, TX

1962 Transferred to Houston, TX by Phillips

1963 Helps build refining, chemical, and petrochemical facilities with Phillips

1966 Quits Phillips; goes to work for Monsanto

1969 Returns to West Texas to work for Ortloff Corporation; involved in building the Rockhouse facility, forty-eight miles northeast of Van Horn, TX

1970 Moves to Midland, TX as a project manager for Ortloff; eventually promoted to Vice President of construction, then Vice President of operations

1975 Establishes Houston office for Ortloff

1982 Ortloff shuts down its Houston operations; Page returns to Odessa; buys majority interests in Ref-Chem

1986 Buys Don Love Inc. in Pasadena, TX and combines it with Ref-Chem

1989 Moves back to Houston to give more direction to Houston branch of Ref-Chem

1997 Returns to Odessa; Says Page of his city-toggling timeline, "People accused me of the seven-year itch—that I've either been in West Texas for seven years or Houston for seven years. And now I've been in Odessa for eleven years and plan to stay! I love West Texas."

1998 Ref-Chem purchases SMC McEver, an engineering & construction company based in Houston, to complement its Houston operation

Just how lucrative this management position was, was most apparent when Page compared it to his three previous years of summer employment. As an engineer-in-training with the state highway department, he had earned only half as much. To supplement this low pay, the college student lifeguarded on the weekends. He also hired himself out to farmers who, happy to squeeze more productivity into each day, paid him to drive their weeding tractors from dinner to midnight. Nevertheless, there was something the engineering job provided that ultimately proved more valuable than money: direction. Helping build Highway 70 across northwestern Kansas was so enjoyable for the young man that he returned to college to pursue a civil engineering degree.

Page graduated from college in 1961. The first part of his career he spent toggling between West Texas and Houston, working for Phillips Petroleum, Monsanto and Ortloff Engineers. He carefully studied the industrial construction business, knowing that when the time was right he would acquire his own company. Page explains the criteria he was looking for in a sale: "The company had to be established with a good reputation. Its management might need to be approaching a retirement stage where they were looking for a change—needing some young blood. It probably had to be a challenging situation for the company at that time or I was not going to be able to afford it because I did not have that much money." Page found just what he was seeking in 1983, in the form of an Odessa-based construction and maintenance company called Ref-Chem. He promptly sold every bit of equity he had to buy a controlling interest in the business.

Sitting in his Chairman/CEO's office twenty-six years after taking leadership of Ref-Chem, Page reflects on the long job history that led him there. He recalls proudly, "I worked from the time I was in the fifth grade, delivering the *Fort Worth Star-Telegram* in Graham, Texas." When his parents divorced and his mom moved him to Oregon, he delivered papers there, too. Then, at twelve years old, Page moved to live with his grandfather in Oakley, Kansas. In that modest farming community, Page found no shortage of work at the pool, the grocery store, and the Sale

Photo courtesy of Hendershot Photography

Barn. The Sale Barn was the town's livestock auction house and Page's job was cutting cattle. "Not castrating cattle," the businessman is quick to clarify, "*separating* cattle into like kinds—using a cutting gate or a horse." Page had experience riding horses thanks to his grandfather, a respected horseman who rode in the Oakley Range Riders drill team. Occasionally, Page would even ride alongside his grandfather in the team's performances. Page considered his grandfather his mentor and sought to follow closely in his footsteps. Consequently, the high-school student tried his hand at ranching, buying some cattle and running it with his grandfather's herd. When a drought beset the area, Page's grandfather was kind enough to pay for all the livestock's feed. Yet, even being spared that expense, Page only broke even when his cattle were sold. Says Page of the humbling experience, "It was obvious I was not going to be rich enough to be a cattleman or farmer."

> "I always tried to instill in my kids at an early age that they needed to work and earn their money."

Page has three children from his first marriage: Donna; Rodney, the Vice President and CFO of Ref-Chem's Houston, Texas, operations; and Bradley, the owner of an appraisal business in the Clear Lake area near Houston. Page observes, "One of my greatest accomplishments is raising my kids and having all three kids graduate from college and be self-supporting and good parents and not giving me a lot of trouble." He reflects for a moment, then adds humbly, "Having said all that, I know a lot of parents that did as good or better job than I've done that have had problems with their kids. I think [raising kids is] probably a lot like being in business—it's about being lucky, having the right timing."

Though Page downplays the effectiveness of his parenting, it's apparent that promoting a good work ethic in his children played no small part in their success. Page explains, "I always tried to instill in them at an early age that they needed to work and earn their money." The kids started working at fourteen and fifteen years old, approximately the same age as their father had. The boys cut lawns and Donna worked in fast food. But just because they were out in the real world working didn't mean they had a real-world grasp on money and its application. Page laughs, "I can remember my daughter going to work at McDonald's and then insisting that *I* help her buy a car because she had a job now." After listening patiently to his daughter's interesting but flawed logic, Page made Donna a deal. He wouldn't *buy* her a car but he would *loan* her the money, without interest, to buy the car and she'd have to reimburse him. He struck the same deal with his sons. To earn the money to pay off their debt, Page's progeny could work around the house and at outside jobs. Also, any good grades the children made would be credited

CAT CRANKERS, LLC.

IN ASSOCIATION WITH

PHB

INDEPENDENT SERVICE CONTRACTOR

432-413-3133

Ad designed by Hunt Advertising.

toward their debt. When college time came around, Page agreed to help with tuition, books, room and board. But if the kids wanted a social life to boot, they'd have to fund it themselves.

Some people, namely today's teenagers, would argue that jobs before adulthood put a damper on one's fun. But Page contends, "I had a great social life when I was a kid. A lot of people feel sorry for me that I *did* have to work, but I think that's one of the best things that ever happened to me."

Another one of the best things that ever happened to him, Page notes fondly, is his wife, Peggy Sue. To her he credits much of his and Ref-Chem's success, saying, "Peggy has brought many blessings to my life, including two more wonderful daughters: Suzette Cole and Pamela Roberts." Page also gratefully acknowledges Ref-Chem's loyal employees, clients, vendors, and community leaders who "have always stepped to the plate to support me in times of need."

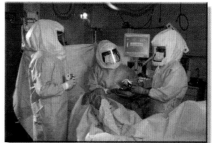

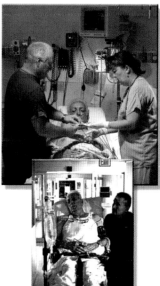

SAULSBURY INDUSTRIES

GROVE

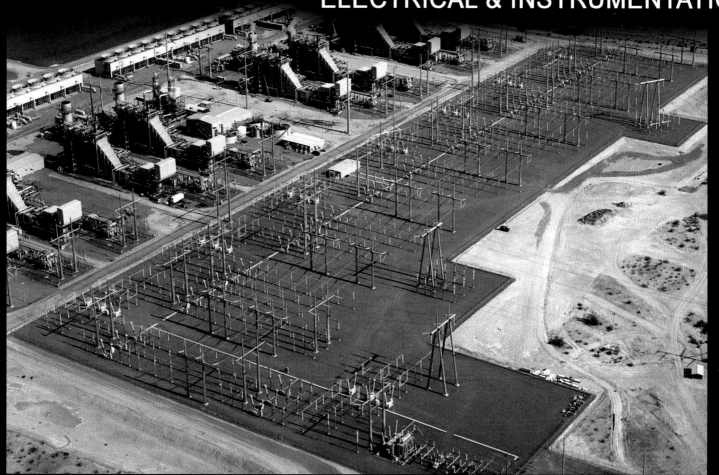

Dick Saulsbury, exhibiting the same one-hundred-percent commitment that shaped Saulsbury Industries, recently lost sixty pounds over six months. Here, he gets his blood flowing bright and early with a rigorous workout at Odessa's World Gym.

Dick Saulsbury accepts a weighted medicine ball from his trainer, Kim Clinkenbeard.

Dick Saulsbury

GIANT COMMITMENT

Until recently, Dick Saulsbury would not enter a restaurant without a packet of ranch dressing nestled in his breast pocket. Years of attending ill-equipped business conventions and dinners had trained him to come prepared. Why not everyone understood the necessity of ranch, Saulsbury hadn't the foggiest, but he had given up trying to correct their ignorance.

Once he had made a big scene in an Austin restaurant after his favorite condiment failed to appear with his seventy-five-dollar meal. The waiter tried to placate him with a tureen of buttermilk, but this ersatz dressing only increased Saulsbury's annoyance. Why was it that the availability of ranch dressing was inversely proportionate to a restaurant's exclusiveness? Saulsbury could do without the restaurant's prim waiters, pressed napkins and pats of chilled butter. Just give him his ranch!

Thus, when ranch dressing was wrested from his diet in 2007, Saulsbury was horrified.

"Why don't you just get a pistol and shoot me!" he protested when his personal trainer proposed a new menu.

Saulsbury had mentioned to his family he wanted to lose weight, but he hadn't anticipated such a zealous response. His children had staged a veritable intervention, commandeering one hour of his time every Monday, Wednesday, and Friday morning to meet with a personal trainer. Saulsbury had agreed to the workouts and nutrition counseling, but he hadn't anticipated this ranch restriction.

"We don't want to have to carry you down the mountain," one of his sons explained, alluding to a big hunting trip scheduled three months later, in October. And it was true; Saulsbury would need to be in top shape for one of his favorite activities. There would be uneven terrain to navigate, hefty packs and rifles to tote, and thinner air to inhale. Saulsbury considered his priorities: He loved hunting; he loved being immersed in nature. Plus, at age sixty-eight, he was finally learning to detach himself from work in favor of family leisure time. He wasn't going to let his weight hinder these activities.

"Alright. No ranch dressing," Saulsbury conceded, and Kim Clinkenbeard smiled.

"Why don't you just get a pistol and shoot me!" he protested

Clinkenbeard is Saulsbury's personal trainer. Though she's seven inches shorter than her client, she has no trouble exerting authority over him in the gym. "See the invisible whip she's got in her hand," Saulsbury jokes as he slides obediently onto a stationary bike. While he furiously pedals, Clinkenbeard stands at his side: hands on hips, eyes closely monitoring the bike's speed.

About her client's newfound commitment to exercise, Clinkenbeard brags, "He's a hundred-percent. You're either [committed] or you're not, and that transfers over into

CAREER HIGHLIGHTS

1961 Moves to Wickett, TX to work for Dixie Electric

1962 Moves to Odessa, TX with Dixie Electric

1964 Starts Star Electric Co. with two partners

1967 Starts Saulsbury Electric

1976 Forms Eagle Instrumentation & Construction

1980 Establishes construction branch named Saulcon

1994 Turns Eagle Instrumentation into Saulsbury Engineering & Construction Inc., which offers turnkey engineering, procurement, and construction services nationwide

1997 Opens Saulcon Inc. and Saulsbury Electric Inc. divisions in Farmington, NM; Saulsbury Industries gains own IT department

2007 Saulsbury Industries surpasses the 1,500-employees mark

all different aspects of your life." Peddling furiously on his stationary bike, Saulsbury interjects, "I should be committed...(wheeze)...to the nuthouse in Big Spring!"

Joking aside, commitment is the key to Saulsbury's widespread success. He's committed to his wife, Amelia, with whom he will soon celebrate forty-nine years of marriage. He's committed to his company, which he grew from Saulsbury Electric in 1967 to the multibranched, multi-state Saulsbury Industries. Moreover, he's a committed Christian, always seeking to do God's will in the world. Saulsbury confesses he's serving on "way too many boards" at the moment. Meals on Wheels, Citizens for Decency, the Ector County Independendent School District's Education Foundation, and The Battalion of Deborah are just a few of the fifteen nonprofits that currently benefit from his dedication and leadership.

By now Saulsbury has broken a sweat. The stationary bike's red LED display reads 19:35. When he began working out six months ago, Saulsbury managed seven minutes on the bike, but now he charges through twenty. Before moving to the next piece of equipment, he opts for a water break. Saulsbury is like Sam Walton when it comes to consumer goods, favoring old clunkers over luxury cars and nondescript sneakers over Nikes. He pejoratively refers to the blue-bottled Dasani in his hand as "fancy water." Clinkenbeard, her mind already on the next task, watches Saulsbury swig the water and asks how long of a break he'll need. Saulsbury's blue eyes twinkle. "How long does it take to drown yourself? That's how long I need," he quips. Both trainer and client smile, knowing his resistance is just for show. Saulsbury quickly rehydrates himself, then ambles good-naturedly to the chest press machine.

Saulsbury isn't new to physical exertion. As a youth, he burned calories unconsciously in the Arkansas oilfields. His family owned about a dozen wells that, while not lucrative, proved rich in education. By age eleven, Saulsbury was already helping "pull" wells, i.e., pull tubing or rods out of wells when pumps malfunctioned. And, even when the family's wells were running smoothly, there was more than enough work from other independents. As a teen, Saulsbury never had a chance to play after-school sports; his evenings and weekends were already committed to well servicing.

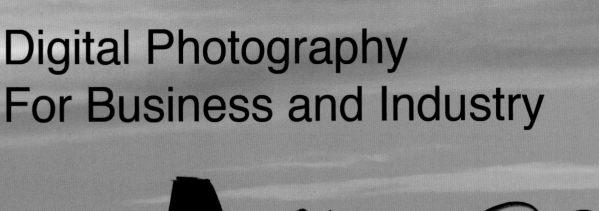

As a young man, Saulsbury took up a more refined type of exercise: adagio. Adagio is the slow, very strenuous part of a ballet duet that features much lifting, balancing and turning. Without a smidge of embarrassment, Saulsbury recounts, "I wore tights and threw girls up in the air." He also enjoyed ballroom dancing. But, the businessman notes, his wife wasn't as fond of cutting a rug so "I danced a thousand dances with her sister." In later years, Saulsbury had a rigorous walking habit until back troubles sidelined him. However, he has one muscle group that's never gone out of commission: "My jaw muscles have always been well-exercised," Saulsbury jokes, acknowledging his reputation as a talker.

"My jaw muscles have always been well-exercised."

After twenty chest presses, sweat has begun to drip from Saulsbury's rosy cheeks into his wispy, white mutton chops. These charmingly anachronistic chops, along with his thoughtful speech, give him the air of an American Founding Father: George Washington at World Gym. This association would undoubtedly please Saulsbury, who avidly reads U.S. history and counts its first president among his favorite personages. From his studies, Saulsbury has concluded that America has strayed far from its republican foundation. So agitated is he by this conclusion, that just thinking about today's governmental policies gives Saulsbury a cardiovascular workout.

But enough of politics for now; it's time for focused abdominal work. Kim rolls out a large, yellow exercise ball and motions for Saulsbury to sit atop it. Saulsbury brightly responds, "Now no one can say I wasn't 'on the ball' today." This makes for a good joke, but it's doubtful that anyone could ever accuse this vim-and-vigor man of being off task. He powers through two sets of twenty crunches, being careful to press his lower back into the ball to prevent injury.

Safety is paramount to Saulsbury, both at the gym and on the job. "Going in business to make a profit is first, but if we can't do it safely, we don't do it," he says. Saulsbury Industries' proprietary safety manual is so comprehensive that several competitors have cribbed it for their own companies. One plagiarist even failed to remove all the Saulsbury Industries references in his reproduction. Saulsbury doesn't begrudge copying for the sake of safety, but he wonders why they didn't just ask him. "We look at a competitor as a competitor, but they can also be a friend," Saulsbury reasons. "Everyone needs to help each other, especially in regards to safety, but everyone wants to be the Lone Ranger." However, Saulsbury adds, there is one scenario where his generosity does not apply: "We've had companies want our safety manual so they could bid against us for a job. That's not right."

Saulsbury is instructed to reposition himself supinely on the exercise ball. Clinkenbeard hands him a ponderous, black medicine ball to pitch and catch above his chest. The trainer stands above him, arms in spot-position, ready to save Saulsbury's nose from any errant throws. "You're limited in commitment till you learn to trust somebody," Saulsbury observes as he confidently lobs the ball up and down.

The connection between commitment and trust is manifest in Saulsbury's own company. By establishing himself early-on as a man of integrity, Saulsbury has attracted and retained a sizeable group of workers. In October 2007, Saulsbury Industries' employees numbered over 1,500, with many boasting ten, twenty, even thirty-plus years of service. Saulsbury's employees are culled from West Texas, then trained, grouped into teams, and sent nationwide to perform turnkey engineering, general construction, and electrical construction. Their services in refining, petrochemical, and gas processing make Saulsbury Industries an important component of the oil and gas industry.

Though visibly fatigued from the medicine ball, Saulsbury follows Clinkenbeard through a final stretching exercise. Saulsbury's docility in the gym is a surprising contrast to the hard-headedness he exhibits in the working world. For example, Saulsbury once hired a consultation company for $28,000, only to dismiss virtually all of their profit-centric advice as incompatible with his goals. But with exercise it's different. Clinkenbeard's goal and Saulsbury's own are the same: an improved quality of life.

Saulsbury has dropped sixty pounds since he began overhauling his health six months ago. Motioning to his midriff, he exclaims proudly, "I'm now wearing 38 [-inch] britches, which I haven't worn in years. I'm fixin' to go to 36." His weight loss has started to turn heads at social gatherings. Women flock to him, admire his attenuated form and ask how they can get their husbands to shape up in the same remarkable way. And then there are the phone calls, at least one a day, from acquaintances wanting to know what magic pill he's taken. No one, of course, likes his answer: that weight loss requires good, old-fashioned self-restraint and one-hundred-percent commitment to a healthier lifestyle.

Today, Saulsbury dresses his salads with light balsamic vinegar. Does it taste as good as ranch? "No. But it's healthier for me and aids digestion," Saulsbury answers pragmatically. Unlike a typical dieter, Saulsbury is unfazed by the thought of his former favorite food. He has a policy of no second-guesses or regrets. Saulsbury concludes matter-of-factly, "Did I have to quit eating ranch dressing? No. But I did."

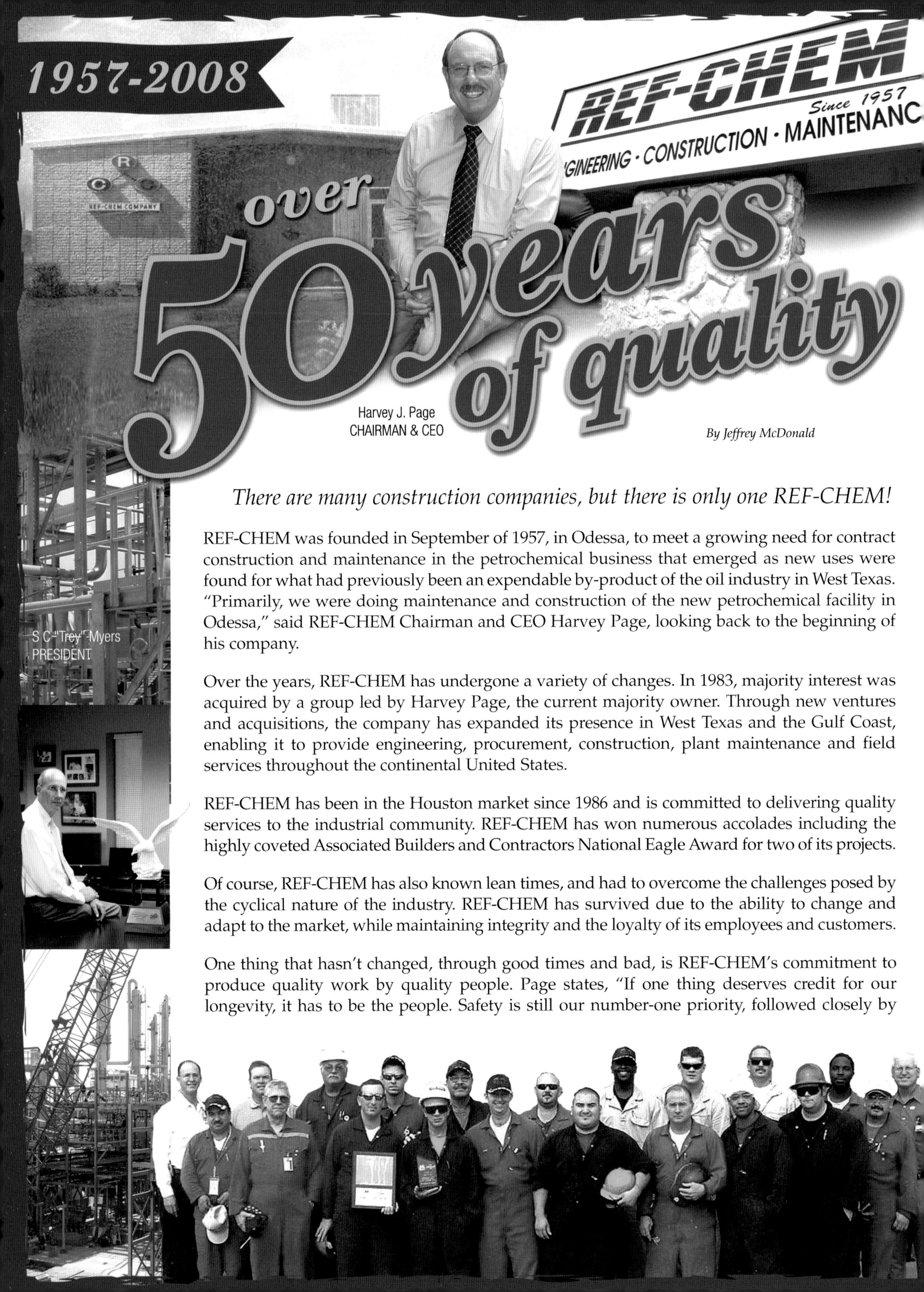

over 50 years of quality

Harvey J. Page
CHAIRMAN & CEO

S C "Trey" Myers
PRESIDENT

By Jeffrey McDonald

There are many construction companies, but there is only one REF-CHEM!

REF-CHEM was founded in September of 1957, in Odessa, to meet a growing need for contract construction and maintenance in the petrochemical business that emerged as new uses were found for what had previously been an expendable by-product of the oil industry in West Texas. "Primarily, we were doing maintenance and construction of the new petrochemical facility in Odessa," said REF-CHEM Chairman and CEO Harvey Page, looking back to the beginning of his company.

Over the years, REF-CHEM has undergone a variety of changes. In 1983, majority interest was acquired by a group led by Harvey Page, the current majority owner. Through new ventures and acquisitions, the company has expanded its presence in West Texas and the Gulf Coast, enabling it to provide engineering, procurement, construction, plant maintenance and field services throughout the continental United States.

REF-CHEM has been in the Houston market since 1986 and is committed to delivering quality services to the industrial community. REF-CHEM has won numerous accolades including the highly coveted Associated Builders and Contractors National Eagle Award for two of its projects.

Of course, REF-CHEM has also known lean times, and had to overcome the challenges posed by the cyclical nature of the industry. REF-CHEM has survived due to the ability to change and adapt to the market, while maintaining integrity and the loyalty of its employees and customers.

One thing that hasn't changed, through good times and bad, is REF-CHEM's commitment to produce quality work by quality people. Page states, "If one thing deserves credit for our longevity, it has to be the people. Safety is still our number-one priority, followed closely by producing quality work, giving our customer true value (an hour's work for an hour's pay) and completing our customer's requirements to help them be successful." This work ethic and dedication to quality services is why ***REF-CHEM is the preferred contractor*** for so many Owners.

REF-CHEM wants to take this opportunity to say ***thank you*** to all its clients, employees, suppliers, subcontractors and community for all their support in making this 50th year celebration possible.

For more information about REF-CHEM or to learn how they can help you with your next project, contact Ben Nichols, Senior Vice President, at 713-477-4471, Mickey Wilson, at 432-332-8531, or visit *www.ref-chem.com*. For employment opportunities with this exceptional company, contact HR at the same number. REF-CHEM is always looking for good people with the right attitude!

For Angie Sims, saving Buster's Well Service required a coup, a court case, and putting her personal credit on the line—getting a tattoo was painless by comparison. Shown here in Midland, Texas's Uprock studio, Sims is being prepped for a "La Patrona" tattoo by owner Sonny Aguilar.

Angie Sims considers her next tattoo. "No Fear" seems a likely candidate.

Angie Sims

GIANT LOYALTY

At the 40th anniversary celebration of Buster's Well Service, the company's general manager exhibited her loyalty in a most unusual way: she flashed her backside at the guests. "If anyone wants this company, they've gotta take a hunk out of my ass to get it!" she bellowed as she tugged down the waistband of her jeans to reveal Buster's logo, tattooed on her right buttock.

Her male employees clapped and hooted. But the second Angie Sims pulled her waistband back up, a disquieting thought entered her head: "What are the employees' wives thinking? Did I offend them?" Then she felt her hand being high-fived. The company wives were swarming around her, slapping her hand and laughing delightedly. No, they weren't offended. They were as elated as Angie that Buster's would stay in the family: not just Sims's family, *their* family—their *company-family*.

Not long before this fete, the company's future had been jeopardized by one of its own. Sims's aunt had inexplicably decided to cash-in her share of the company. It was 2003 and Buster's 40th anniversary. The oil industry and, consequently, Buster's profits were on an upswing. Plus, her aunt and six other shareholders had just staged a successful coup against the company's unscrupulous inheritor. All things considered, Buster's was in good shape.

The aunt's reasoning was arguably flawed, and her method even more so. She sought out a third-party buyer instead of giving her fellow shareholders first chance to purchase. When Sims learned that her aunt had entered a verbal agreement with a prospective buyer, she was appalled. But, unsure of the recourses available to her, she grudgingly took the aspiring purchaser on a tour of the facilities.

"If anyone wants this company, they've gotta take a hunk out of my ass to get it!"

Buster's Well Service is based in Kermit, a West Texas town with less than six thousand residents. Not surprisingly, rumors of the company's crisis were cropping up everywhere: at the grocery store, at the dry cleaners. To prevent her workforce from panicking, Sims called her men together and told it to them straight: "An outsider wants to buy the company and he says he can offer more employee benefits than we can. What do you want us to do?" The men, loyal even after-death to her grandfather Buster, shook their heads stubbornly. Sims wanted to feel heartened by their support, but she feared her employees were acting hastily. She added, "You don't have to decide right now. You can go home and discuss this with your wives." The men replied firmly, "We don't need to go home and talk to our wives. We'll sign our names right now. We want to stay with you." Bewildered, Sims asked, "But what if we go bankrupt?" An employee fixed her straight in the eye and answered, "Then we will walk out that gate and lock it with you." Sims, a woman not easily felled by emotion, found her eyes welling up. She rushed to her office in tears.

CAREER HIGHLIGHTS

1963 Sims's grandfather Buster Crabtree starts Buster's Well Service

1995 Receives share of Buster's Well Service on her thirtieth birthday

1997 Buster passes away

1999 Challenges Buster's corrupt General Manager

2000 Assumes General Manager position

2002 Buster's rejoins the Association of Energy Service Companies (AESC)

2003-2005 Acts as a national AESC HR committee chairperson

2003 Gets million-dollar loan, buys out several shareholding defectors; Buster's featured in *Oil & Gas Report* of the *Midland Reporter Telegram*

2004-2008 Buys six new rigs, the first new rigs for Buster's in twenty years

2006 Assumes Chair of AESC's Permian Basin Chapter

2007 Buys fleet of thirteen trucks and dog houses; Buster's Well Service named "Business of the Year" by Kermit Chamber of Commerce

2008 Buys new rig and dedicates it to Grandpa Buster, giving it his radio call number, 100; Buster's celebrates its 45th anniversary

Sims reflected. She had spent the last four years restoring her grandfather's company to its former glory. It was her baby. Her grandmother Nell Crabtree had bequeathed it to her, her brothers, and her cousins. She would fight for her family's legacy.

First, she had to get her aunt to retract her sale offer. Fortunately, the company's bylaws were on Sims's side and the aunt was constrained to offer her share to Buster's first. But then, two other shareholder-relatives followed the aunt's suit. Now Sims faced a new predicament: how to buy back three of the seven remaining shares.

Kermit's lending institutions had been wary of Buster's ever since Sims's uncle, the aforementioned inheritor, cut bad checks to his employees. Unable to get a loan in her hometown, she solicited help from a bank in Midland, Texas. When her banker Fred McCann called a few days later and asked, "Angie, are you sitting down?" Sims's heart sank into her steel-toed boots. "Yes, sir," she answered fearfully. He continued, "I'm not sure I know how to tell you this, but you're now one million dollars in debt." Sims shrieked in joyous relief. She giddily hung up the phone, hopped in her truck and drove to the company yard. Coming upon her seasoned rig pusher, Chilo, she stopped the truck and ran to him shouting, "We got the loan!" Chilo's eyes moistened and he hugged her hard.

Sims and her company-family weren't given long to rejoice, however. The thwarted buyer slapped a lawsuit on Buster's, as well as Sims personally, for 2.3 million dollars. He sued for the price he would've paid to purchase the company ($1.9 million) and what he felt was his due for waiting on a deal that never materialized. The suits plagued Sims for a year before proceeding to mediation. Finally, the plaintiff settled for $130,000 cash and slunk away.

The year 2003 wasn't the first hard year for Sims. When her share of Buster's Well Service came out of trust in 1995, the company was fading along with her grandfather's health. Sims's grandfather Buster Crabtree was a traditionalist who put his faith in male progeny. When Buster passed away from cancer in 1997, the company's management fell to his only son. For several years the heir went unchecked by family-shareholders, several of whom were still under thirty and unable to control

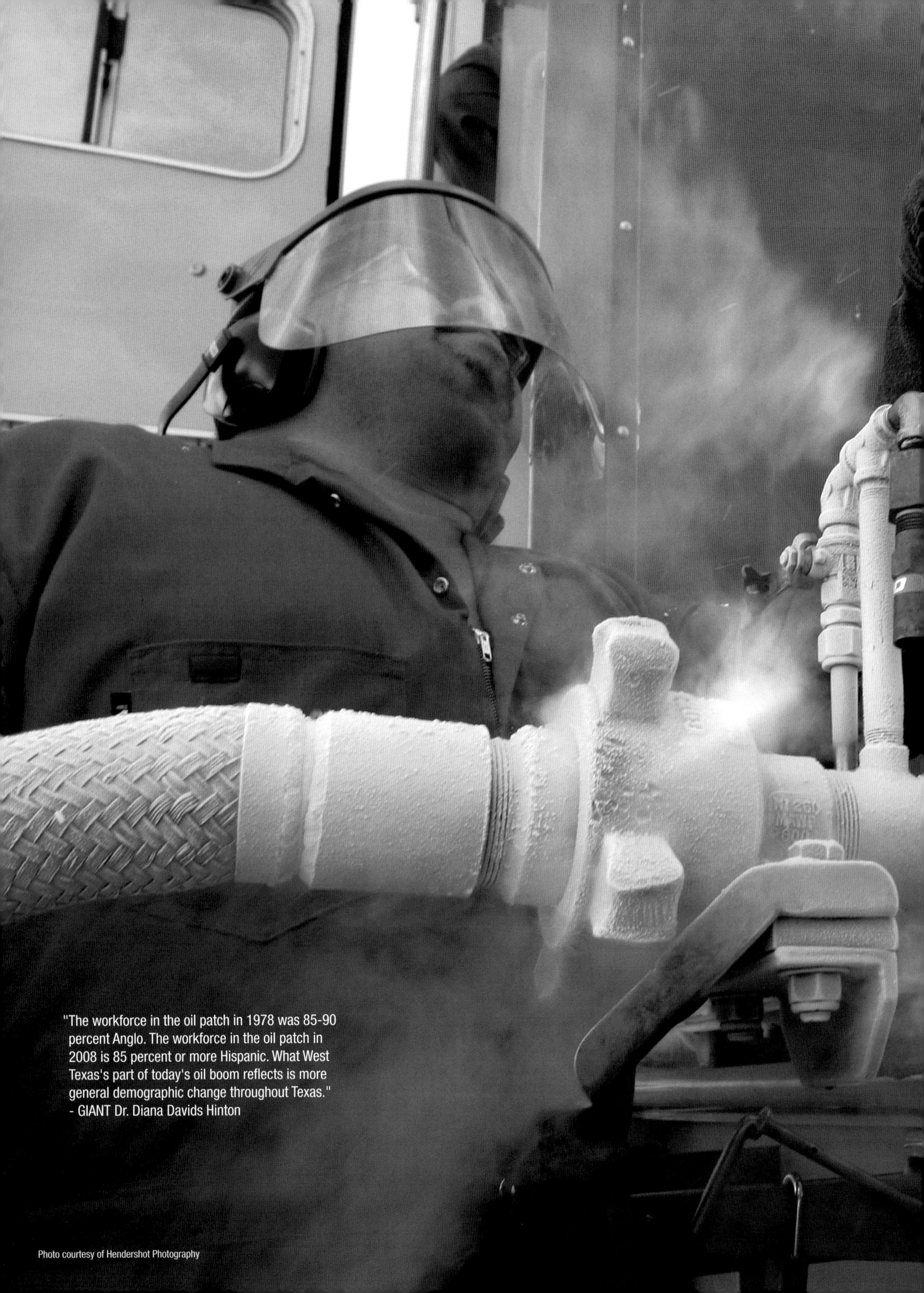

"The workforce in the oil patch in 1978 was 85-90 percent Anglo. The workforce in the oil patch in 2008 is 85 percent or more Hispanic. What West Texas's part of today's oil boom reflects is more general demographic change throughout Texas."
- GIANT Dr. Diana Davids Hinton

Photo courtesy of Hendershot Photography

their own interests. But by 1999, thirty-four-year-old Angie was ready to take her inheritance seriously. She suspected something was amiss in her uncle's business dealings, so she requested the company's administrative documents. After some hemming and hawing, the corporate attorney grudgingly turned over copies of the company's bylaws and meeting notes to Sims. She discovered her uncle had usurped all shareholder positions, dubbing himself President, Vice President, Secretary, and Treasurer. Miffed, she made a note of when the next annual shareholders' meeting was scheduled.

"If I have to go to Hell with my back broken, yes, your checks will clear the bank."

On the day of the next shareholders' meeting, Sims strode into Buster's, brandishing seven proxies for her seven shareholding relatives. Her first order of business: to undo her uncle's monopoly of power. To her aunt she gave the presidency; to her mother, Jessie Shelton, the vice presidency; and to herself, secretary/treasurer. Sims also took on a full-time position as the company's bookkeeper.

Sims vividly remembers her first day of work: "The day that I walked in and introduced myself to the men, it was six-thirty in the morning. These poor guys didn't know Buster had a granddaughter. All they see is this white girl walking in who says, 'I'm one of the owners. I'll be working here every day. I'll be taking care of the books.'" The work-worn men appraised her solemnly. She braced herself for their protestations, but none came. Having been grossly mismanaged for several years, the employees had only one question: "Are our checks going to clear the bank?" Sims squared her jaw and vowed, "If I have to go to Hell with my back broken, yes, your checks will clear the bank."

It turned out Sims would indeed have to go to Hell to keep her promise: Financial Hell. She found the company's office snowed under with bills. Checks were attached to the bills, but they were unsigned and eighteen months overdue. It was a gut-wrenching discovery. Sims recalls, "I don't think there was a thing we didn't owe. The diesel and oil-products bill [alone] was $275,000. That one I almost choked on."

Sims bravely began cleaning the mess. She charged up all her credit cards to pay off some of the outstanding debts. Her aunt also stepped up, using her own finances to back a company loan. Sims then composed a letter to all Buster's vendors and creditors, introducing herself and apologizing for "making them be our bankers." Drawing on her grandfather's reputation for integrity, Sims promised she'd settle every account. Furthermore, if they could give her a set amount of time to honor the debt, any future

money-owed would be paid within thirty days. Sims recalls how she literally laid her life on the line: "I didn't eat. I didn't sleep. I became a chronic smoker. I lost twenty pounds."

In 2000, after eight months as the company's bookkeeper and secretary, Sims took over as General Manager. Her corrupt uncle was long gone, but Buster's still wasn't in the black. "The second time that I signed payroll checks," Sims remembers, "three employees' wives came in because their husbands' checks had not cleared. That scared me more than anything: that these three women came in and said, 'Because your check bounced, I can't feed my family.'" Deeply chagrined, Sims pulled out her personal checkbook and wrote the women new checks. From that incident onward, the morale among Buster's men was markedly improved. And Sims felt better herself. "From that point forward, I had set the bar and I had to reach it."

The actions Sims took to reach that bar were many: First, she restored boundaries, respect, and order to Buster's crews. Next, she acquired loans to replace the old ramshackle equipment. Then, she instituted an effective new safety policy that held an entire rig team responsible for each member's accident. She always humbled herself before clients and employees alike, admitting her ignorance of oil field work and listening to their advice. And, when the opportunity arose, she even donned a uniform, clambered up a rig and cleaned it by herself, proving she wouldn't ask her men to do anything she wouldn't do.

Sims is a tough broad, but she attributes the resuscitation of Buster's to something much greater than her own moxie: her family. By family, the general manager means both her biological family and her honorary family of fifty-something loyal employees. The former is comprised of Angie's mother, Jessie Shelton, and Angie's two brothers, Ty Miller and Mike Sims. The three relatives co-own Buster's with Sims and are her steadfast supporters. Mike Sims also acts as the company's consultant on technical issues. Of her other family, Sims gushes, "The one thing I truly cherish is they've allowed me to earn their respect, be their leader, and also be part of their family. It's a wonderful, gratifying experience when an employee brings in a photo of a new baby or grandbaby, or the baby itself. I've got the best employees." To show her the feeling is mutual, these employees address Sims lovingly as "La Patrona," Spanish's feminine form of "The Boss."

In 2007, the Kermit Chamber of Commerce named Buster's Well Service "Business of the Year." Later that year, Sims received an even more gratifying award: a custom-made plaque from her staff calling her "the boss of the millennium."

THE WARREN COMPANIES

Established in 1971 with the creation of Compressor Systems, Inc., Warren Equipment Company has grown from four employees to over two thousand - from a single company to eight.

From the beginning, each company was built on a commitment to quality, reliability and strong customer service. That commitment is still integral today. The Warren companies provide products and service representing world class manufacturers like Caterpillar, Ariel, Frick, Perkins, Altronic, and Flowserve, just to name a few.

We are dedicated to the delivery and service of these products around the corner and around the globe. This commitment guarantees the best value for our customers. Put the Warren difference to work for you.

WORLD CLASS EMPLOYEES
DELIVERING WORLD CLASS PRODUCTS
SUPPORTED BY WORLD CLASS SERVICE.

www.warren-equipment.com

Service

WARREN
CAT

CSI
Compressor
Systems, Inc.

isc
Ignition Systems & Controls, L.P.

NORAM
POWER SYSTEMS

PSI
Pump Systems
International

PERKINS
SOUTH PLAINS

RCSI
ROTARY COMPRESSOR SYSTEMS INC.

Don Sparks gives a last minute pep talk to his grandson Garrett before the ten-year-old takes the field as part of Midland's 2008 Northern All-Star team. Sparks, his eleven grandkids' number-one fan, attends up to four Little League games a week.

Sparks mimics a batter's pose to the great amusement of his grandson Garrett, who yells stance advice from off-camera.

Don Sparks

GIANT YOUTH ADVOCATE

Don Sparks struggled to keep his feathered headdress aloft in the whipping Lubbock wind. Dust from a nearby cotton field was pelting his glasses and sticking to his war paint. Through the smoldering haze of campfire sparks he could just make out his friend Jimmy Floyd. Floyd, decked out in similar Native American regalia, raised his hand for silence.

The Indian Guides, obeying their fourth aim, "to listen while others speak," noisily shooshed each other. Close to a hundred headbanded boys, ages five to ten, were present in the clearing. Those seated farther away from the fire shivered at the plummeting temperature and nestled deeper into their fathers' sides. The dads had assembled a hundred miles from home to celebrate the induction of a new Longhouse Council for their Midland Nation. The boys, on the other hand, had come mainly for the promised after-party of hot dogs, s'mores and a sleepover.

The YMCA's Indian Guide program was begun in 1926 to facilitate quality one-on-one time between fathers and sons. For the boys, it's an opportunity to watch their fathers in leadership positions. For the men, it's a way to model for their children the right way to interact in a community. Each tribe has eight to twelve families and is responsible for organizing its own activities, crafts, and games at monthly meetings. The National Council arranges four out-of-town campouts each year.

Like all Y-Indian Guide events, this evening's opened with the pledge. At the presiding Nation Chief's signal, a chorus of male voices chanted solemnly, "We, father and son, through friendly service to each other…(the wind howled)…to our family, to this tribe…(the tents pulled at their stakes)…to our community, seek a world…(the campfire snapped loudly)…pleasing to the eye of the Great Spirit." Lightning was glimmering in the distance, but the incumbent Chief pushed on with the agenda. Raising his voice above the meteorological commotion, he announced the new roster: Scout, Pathfinder, Wampum Bearer, Tally Keeper, Sandpainter…When he named the new Medicine Man, Don Sparks smiled and handed over his medicine bag.

Fathers hoisted sons into the crooks of their arms like footballs and charged toward their minivans.

Chief Floyd cleared his throat and looked nervously up at the ever-darkening sky. He began, "Finally, I'm proud to hand my 'coup stick' over to the Council's newest Nation Chief, Don Sp...," but was silenced by a prodigious thunderclap. The ensuing raindrops extinguished the campfire and the swirling wind made quick work of collapsing the tents. Fathers hoisted sons into the crooks of their arms like footballs and charged toward their minivans. A few minutes later, many were on the road—a water-logged caravan heading south.

Floyd has never let his successor forget that campout; he loves to rib Sparks with: "The minute I turned it over to you, things went to pot!" Sparks's sons are similarly loath to

Photo courtesy of Hendershot Photography

CAREER HIGHLIGHTS

1962 Graduates from University of Texas at Austin with a petroleum engineering degree

1962-1965 Active Service in U.S. Navy

1965-1969 Exploitation Engineer, Reservoir Engineer for Shell Oil Company

1969-1971 District Engineer Freeport Oil Company, directs drilling and production operations in West Texas, New Mexico, Oklahoma, and the Rocky Mountain area

1971-1973 Consulting Engineer with Midland, TX consulting firm

1973 Starts Discovery Operating with friend Ernest Angelo, along with private consulting

1974 Volunteers as Nation Chief for Midland's Y-Indian Guides program

1980 Combines consulting businesses with college friend Ronny Platt to form Platt, Sparks & Associates Consulting Petroleum Engineers in Austin and Midland

1983 Oldest son, Jeff, joins Discovery Operating and is followed by his two brothers over the next few years

1997-2001 Takes turns with sons and Fred Brown going to the Ukraine, evaluating for the Ukraine President how to get the Ukraine's oil industry back online

1979-1990 and **1994-1998** Committee Member Midland Young Life, a non-denominational program sharing the Good News with high-school kids

1990-Present Board Member at Manor Park

1999-2003 Independent Petroleum Association of America (IPAA) Board Member for the Texas Permian Region

1999-2007 Executive Board IPAA

2003 Receives IPAA Leadership Award

put the story to rest. Their dad chuckles, "My boys like to remind me that we had storms on the campouts the *whole year* I was Chief." Weather disturbances aside, the oilman considers his reign as Midland, Texas's Nation Chief to have been a very positive experience, yielding both immediate and long-term rewards. "There are a lot of blessings that come from that [program]," reflects Sparks, "A lot of those boys are back in Midland today with their own kids. It's a highlight to get to see young men that you worked with, grow up, become good citizens themselves, and become a part of the community."

"We had storms on the campouts the whole year I was Chief."

After fourth grade, the final year of Indian Guides, Sparks and his sons had no problem finding other ways to keep busy. There was at least one sport for every season. And Sparks, taking advantage of the flexible schedule that business ownership affords, made a point to be involved in all of them. He coached Little League for twelve years, football for ten years, and even basketball for a spell. The rare times that he wasn't coaching, he was in the stands, pumping his fist encouragingly and yelling praise to every kid on the team. Using sports as a teaching point, Sparks drilled into his sons and their teammates lessons in respect, discipline, determination, teamwork, self-esteem, courage and good sportsmanship.

Despite innumerable practices, tournaments, and trophies, none of Sparks's sons proceeded on to professional sports. They did, however, hit upon an occupation that makes their father very proud. Today, all three sons, Jeff, Kevin, and Todd, are partners in their father's oil business Discovery Operating. The patriarch cheerfully admits, "They can run Discovery Operating without me, but I appreciate the opportunity to continue to be involved."

Once his boys took hold of Discovery's reigns, Sparks found more freedom in his schedule. Thus, when an unexpired term

Save the wells!
1-800-299-8105
TEXAS – NEW MEXICO – OKLAHOMA – KANSAS - COLORADO
REEF
The Chemical Industry's Problem Solvers

2004 Runs in Special Election, Unexpired Term for Texas Senate District 31; loses to Kel Seliger

2006 Receives Hearst Energy Award for Lifetime Achievement in the Oil and Gas Industry

2006 Honored as a Distinguished Graduate at The College of Engineering at the University of Texas at Austin

2007-2008 Board President of Live on Stage! Community Concerts of Midland

opened in the Texas Senate in 2004, some of Sparks's business friends urged him to campaign. However, it wasn't until an even more influential group approached him that the oilman gave in. "When your sons come up to you and say, 'We think you should run,' well…," Sparks shrugs and opens his hands in a "what can you do?" expression. After all, the businessman had spent many a family dinner on his imaginary soapbox, enumerating societal needs and suggesting solutions. What kind of role model would he be if he didn't take part in the opportunity to offer governmental input?

Sparks had served on Midland's public school board and volunteered in a variety of local organizations. But he viewed this election partly as a chance to take his youth advocacy to a higher level—to reach more children, via state-wide policy, than he had in those years of city powwows. And, were Sparks to reach the Senate floor, he knew the first issue he'd push: lowering the high-school dropout rate. Though he avoids the term "vocational training" with its negative cast, Sparks proposes a new curriculum for non-college-bound students who have a technical bent. Sounding for a moment like Sidney Poitier's passionately pragmatic character in *To Sir With Love*, Sparks urges, "Teach them life skills—how to make a budget—we are losing a lot of young people and yet we [society] need them." Applying his vision to the West Texas economy in particular, he continues, "We need good, skilled people in the [oil and gas] industry who may not have college educations. We need skilled labor who are willing to be in the field, who understand how to properly handle a well, service wells, run logs, run frac' treatments." Sparks concludes adamantly, "We're letting these kids drop out of school when they could have really gainful employment—the opportunity to make really good salaries."

Sparks attributes part of the dropout problem to the public school system's reticence to educate students about alternatives to college. In today's higher-learning-geared curriculum, it's easy for students who are not university-bound to think high school holds nothing for them. This phenomenon is particularly frustrating to Sparks, who credits his own career course to a

"Out in the oil field wrestling that steel is very, very heavy work. When you're a roughneck, you suffer from chronic fatigue." - GIANT Nick Taylor

Photo courtesy of Hendershot Photography

teacher-guided exploration of employment options. It was the eighth grade, and Sparks and his classmates were instructed to research and write about a handful of potential careers. Sparks chose ranching and farming and oil and gas. He explains, "The reason I looked at oil and gas was that there was a nitroglycerin shooter that came into the hotel where I worked." Sparks's dad owned a dry cleaning shop in the Herring Hotel in Amarillo, and one of the young Sparks's chores was to deliver the shooter's dry-cleaned clothes to his room. Of the mysterious man, Sparks recalls, "He was a pretty wild and wooly fellow—but I tell you what—he had the nicest clothes…when he was in the hotel…everybody talked about what he did and it was very exciting talk." However, in the course of writing his school paper, Sparks learned shooting was only glamorous if you lived long enough to spend your money. Sparks says wryly, "When I did my research, I realized that handling nitro, walking around and dropping it into holes wasn't exactly what I wanted to do because not everybody survived that long." Fortunately, while researching nitroglycerin shooting, the young man learned about running rigs and lowering casing—now those activities sounded more exciting and a lot less lethal to Sparks. He set his goal. When the young man entered the University of Texas at Austin four years later, the excitement those oil field stories had stirred in him bubbled anew as he began the challenge of earning a petroleum engineering degree.

"I realized that handling nitro, walking around and dropping it into holes wasn't exactly what I wanted to do."

Sparks's 2004 political platform focused on the school system, agriculture, and water conservation. He ran against six other candidates and placed third in the polls. The victor was fellow Republican Kel Seliger. When asked about the loss, Sparks grins amiably, "It was an experience—let's put it that way—and not a bad experience." Though it probably would've been nice to hold political office, Sparks seems content with the fact that he tried. It's just like he told his sons in Little League—and like his sons told him years later when the Senate seat came open: "You need to step up to the plate and swing the bat."

THE FIRST HOME OFFICE OF THE SIGNAL OIL & GAS COMPANY

"I guess I have sort of an obsession," admits Nick Taylor of his Rayo lamp collection. But, in his defense, could there be a more appropriate light by which to read all those Rockefeller biographies?

Nick Taylor

GIANT BIBLIOPHILE

"Once a Rayo user, always one" is an advertising slogan that, though it originated in the early twentieth century, aptly describes twenty-first-century Nick Taylor. Taylor, a lawyer and oilman, has been collecting Rayo oil lamps for over thirty years. He's fascinated with them, not so much for their appearance or function, as for their association with America's first capitalist giant.

John D. Rockefeller, through his Standard Oil Company, patented the Rayo lamp in 1906. Aesthetically speaking, the Rayo is rather unremarkable with its plain, nickel-plated brass base and opaque white shade. Economically speaking, though, the Rayo is nothing short of extraordinary. By mass-producing a simple-to-operate table lamp at a low price, Rockefeller cleverly converted America, one household at a time, into a loyal consumer of his Standard lamp oil.

Taylor loves Rayo lamps because they signify smart thinking in business. Another example of Rockefeller's genius that Taylor appreciates is the former's scrutiny of details. In the early 1870s, J.D. Rockefeller visited a New York City Standard Oil plant and observed a machine soldering a cap on a five-gallon tin can of kerosene. Rockefeller asked the resident expert how many drops of solder were used to secure each lid. When the worker answered "Forty," Rockefeller suggested he try thirty-eight drops. At thirty-eight some of the seals failed, but at thirty-nine drops the caps were leak-free. The machines' dispensation of solder was tweaked accordingly. By saving one drop per lid, Rockefeller estimated he saved $2,500 the first year and, ultimately, hundreds of thousands of dollars.

"I like to stand back and study things carefully."

By following a similar formula in which productivity is maximized and inefficiency minimized, Taylor has achieved prodigious growth in his own company. Taylor estimates his Mexco Energy Corporation's assets are now forty times greater than they were when he purchased the company in 1983. The businessman attributes his success to a lifelong habit of observation before action. "I like to stand back and study things carefully. I watched successful oilmen while I practiced law; I saw what was successful and not successful." In addition to watching his contemporaries, Taylor absorbed book after book about the oil industry and its luminaries.

"The most influential biography I've read is a book called *Only to God*, a biography of a man named Cabot." Godfrey Lowell Cabot (1861-1962) began his career as a chemist but soon became a powerful industrialist. His early experimentation with carbon black, a by-product of gas field development, led to his purchasing of Pennsylvania gas fields. Taylor elaborates, "Cabot found gas fields too remote to be connected to cities. He built carbon black plants that would burn the gas to produce carbon black for inks and dyes." By the late 1880s the carbon black market was weak from over-production, so Cabot switched his focus to natural gas as a product in itself. Taylor recalls, "I was impressed that Cabot used his skill as a chemist in oil.

Ad designed by Hunt Advertising.

CAREER HIGHLIGHTS

1959 Graduates from Harvard with degree in government; officer/ paratrooper in U.S. Army Infantry

1960-1963 Attends Georgetown Law School; passes bar

1964-1965 Post-grad studies in oil and gas law and taxation at Southern Methodist University

1965-1970 Works for Sherman & Sterling in New York as associate attorney, handles international (e.g., Algeria, Venezuela, Canada) deals, everything from oil and gas tax audits to mergers and acquisitions and financings and company startups

1966 Participates in twenty-one wells, of which twenty were producers, in Haskell County, TX

1970-1974 Associate Attorney for Locke Purnell Firm in Dallas, TX

1974-1993 Partner in Stubbeman, McRae, Sealy, Laughlin, & Browder of Midland, TX

1983 Buys control of public company Mexco Energy Corporation

1993 Leaves law firm to build up Mexco Energy

2003 Mexco listed on American Stock Exchange; Mexco's CFO, Tammy McComic, rings the opening bell

Present Taylor's pursuing his goal of getting Mexco on the NY Stock Exchange

I thought, 'Gee, maybe I can use law as an entry point into the oil and gas business.'" Thus, after attaining a law degree from Georgetown, Taylor proceeded to Southern Methodist University for post-graduate studies in oil and gas law and taxation.

By 1966, Taylor had finished his post-graduate studies and was a practicing lawyer. He was also participating in twenty-one oil wells in Haskell County, Texas, twenty of which were producers. Prior to these investments, Taylor's involvement with the oil industry had been physical rather than financial. Several years earlier, he had spent a summer toiling for Empire Drilling Company as a roughneck. At the time, Empire was drilling wells for Sun Oil Company in Louisiana. Taylor remembers, "One of the roughnecks had a station wagon with no doors or seatbelts. We had to lock arms around the open windows to hold on. He charged us a dollar a day to drive us to the rig." But a car could only take the workers so far. The last swampy leg of the journey required the roughnecks to switch from steel-toed boots to sneakers and sploosh through the sucking mud. The roughnecks worked eight hours a day, seven days a week. Taylor had previously worked in heavy construction, but an oil worker's level of exertion was new to him. "Out in the oil field wrestling that steel is very, very heavy work. When you're a roughneck, you suffer from chronic fatigue." Yet Taylor thoroughly enjoyed the job. "We were drilling nine-thousand-foot wells. Our crew was the fastest. We'd always get the roundtrips—pull all the pipe out and run it back in." His eyes brighten with the memory, "The exciting roar of the engines, the clank of the steel—we made a well every time we drilled." With satisfaction, he concludes, "It was a good way to learn about the industry."

The last swampy leg of the journey required the roughnecks to sploosh through the sucking mud.

For Taylor, who toggled between judicial and industrial realms as a young man, the autobiography *Thomas Mellon and His Times* would have been a treasure chest of tips. In it the nineteenth-century Irish immigrant recounts his development from farmer's son to urbane businessman. Mellon began his career as a lawyer, but his simultaneous activity as an investor proved more lucrative. After thirty years as an esteemed jurist, Mellon moved full-time into finance in 1869 as the founder of T. Mellon and Sons Bank. This private lending institution would append its name to a number of history-making ventures, including the revolutionary oil gusher Spindletop. In his memoir, the Mellon-family patriarch explicitly stated that his writings were for relatives' eyes only. Thus, although it was printed in 1885, Mellon's history was not published publicly and in-full until 1994—too late for Taylor's foray into petroleum. Laments Taylor, "I wish I could have read that book sooner, I probably would've moved [from law to oil] sooner."

When asked to estimate the volume of his personal library, Taylor makes an expansive gesture and explains, "I've read a tremendous number of biographies—whether on companies or people. I've read the history of Standard Oil of California, history of Royal Dutch Shell, the history of Mid-America Pipeline Company—I could go on naming them for hours." Notably, Taylor does more for the nonfiction industry than just avidly consume its publications. He also lends a critical eye to some of its nascent works. As a respected friend of oil field historian Dr. Diana Hinton, Taylor has been asked on several occasions to look over her books' galleys. Hinton reports that Taylor, with his knowledge of legislative history, was of especial help for her book about fraudulent oil promoters of the 1920s, *Easy Money*. But Taylor has a more self-effacing way of describing his scholarly input: "They were often light comments because I think she had it perfectly."

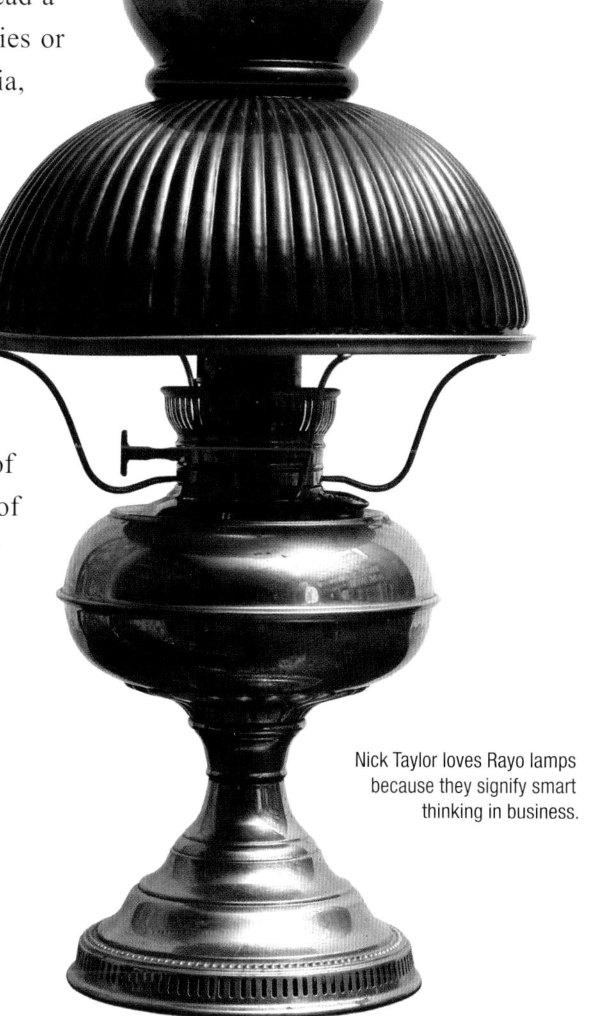

Nick Taylor loves Rayo lamps because they signify smart thinking in business.

Photos were taken by Hendershot Photography in 2001 at the wedding celebration of Williams's son Clayton Wade.

Clayton Williams belts out one of his favorite ballads, "El Papalote," with help from Dorothy Garcia and Mariachi Fortuna de Raymond Flores. Though the song is a chest-puffing assertion of masculine independence, Williams is admittedly a softie when it comes to his wife, Modesta.

The sparks between Modesta and Clayton have been flying since 1964.

Clayton W. Williams Jr.

GIANT PERSONALITY

"Why don't cha play some real music?" jeered a restaurant patron, his breath stale with beer and refried beans. The mariachi band performing a few tables away squirmed uncomfortably. "Why don't cha shut your mouth?" fired back the now-famous Clayton Williams Jr.

But back then, in 1963, everyone at the Monterrey Kitchen just knew Williams as "that guy from Fort Stockton who comes in every Thursday and sings with the mariachis." The mariachis were Williams's friends and he wasn't going to let some inebriate disparage them. He eagerly clenched his fist and watched the bully charge. When the drunk came close enough, Williams greeted him with a prodigious punch. "You gotta get the first punch: I learned that as a boy," the oilman explains as he recalls how his opponent went flying across the tiny restaurant.

"That shickled the tit out of me!"

An all-out brawl erupted. The mariachi-heckler butted Williams into a table, busting the table and throwing Williams on his back. From this supine position, the wily Williams managed a surprise attack. He locked his legs like a vice around his opponent's torso, then pummeled him with both fists till the man's white shirt glistened red. By now the cafe owner's hand was hovering over the phone, threatening to call the police. The fighters weren't interested in getting arrested so they reluctantly disengaged. The drunk was marched home by his much-chagrined wife and Williams slid jauntily back into his booth. The bully returned to the restaurant later that night: bathed, bandaged and badly humbled. Williams hoots with glee as he recalls the man's mirthless reentrance, "That shickled the tit out of me!"

Though Williams had returned to his seat the unquestionable victor, his date was less than impressed. It was clear, even to the battle-high Williams, that there would be no second date with this girl. But, as it turned out, this date didn't really matter. The real love of his life was seated just a few booths away and her pretty brown eyes had seen everything.

The next time Modesta Simpson saw her future husband, it was a year later at the same little Mexican eatery. Williams was once again putting on a show, but this time the Kitchen found his antics easier to tolerate. There he was, a short, scrappy oil-lease broker singing with the restaurant's mariachi band. No other gringo could belt out those ballads so feelingly. "*No soy papalote de ninguna mujer,*" he thumped his chest proudly, *I'm not the kite of any woman!* He swaggered about, singing line after line about masculine independence. Then, for a finale, he dropped to his knees as if the pathos of the lyrics had become too much to bear. He didn't arise until the last note finished reverberating off the restaurant's near-bare walls. Then, flashing his trademark Cheshire-cat grin, he bowed to the audience. What a showman.

Williams has been singing these Mexican folk ballads, or *corridos*, since he was a boy. As ambitious in youth as he would be in manhood, Williams leased a cotton farm at age

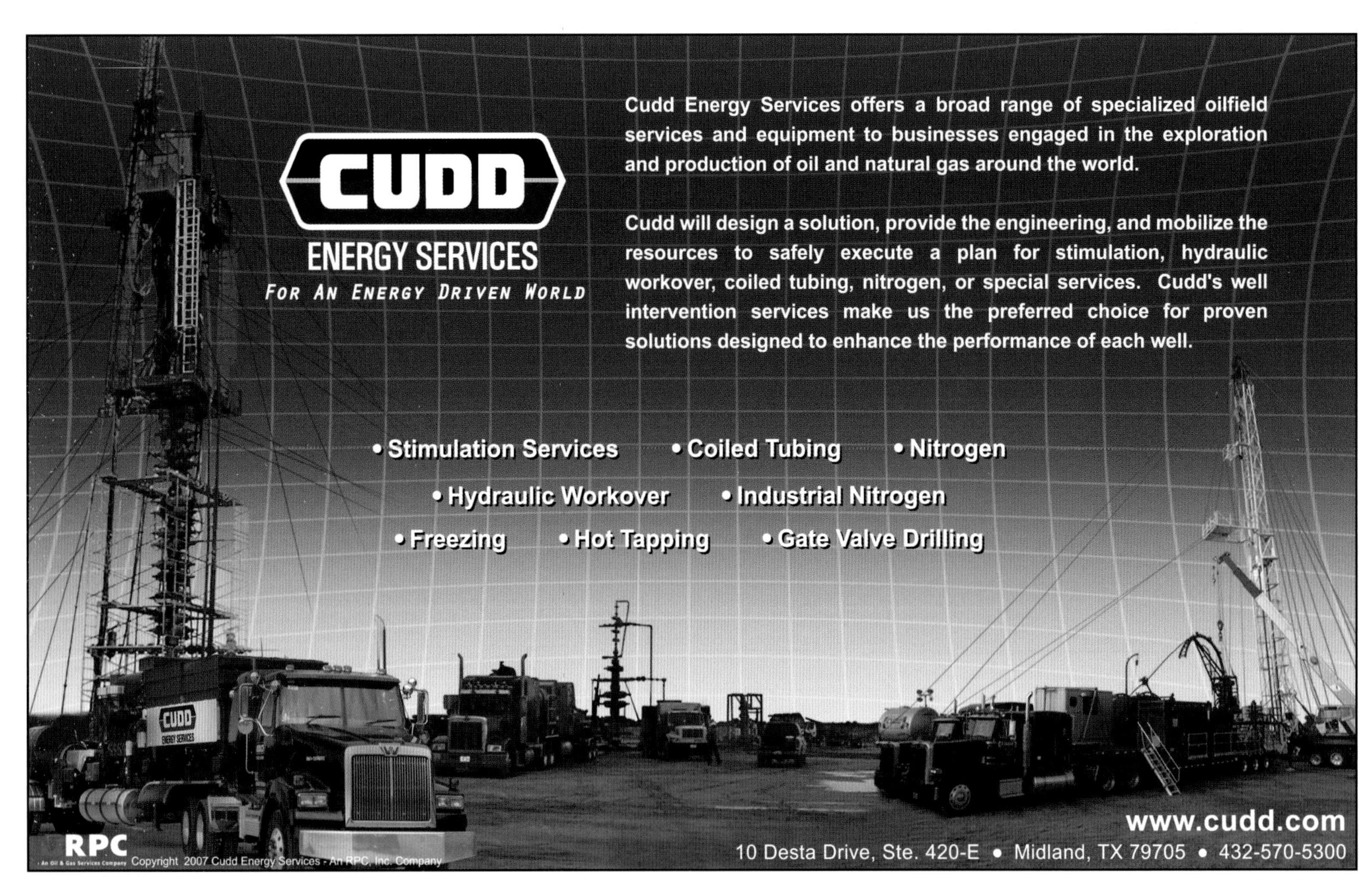
CUDD
ENERGY SERVICES
FOR AN ENERGY DRIVEN WORLD
Cudd Energy Services offers a broad range of specialized oilfield services and equipment to businesses engaged in the exploration and production of oil and natural gas around the world.
Cudd will design a solution, provide the engineering, and mobilize the resources to safely execute a plan for stimulation, hydraulic workover, coiled tubing, nitrogen, or special services. Cudd's well intervention services make us the preferred choice for proven solutions designed to enhance the performance of each well.
• Stimulation Services • Coiled Tubing • Nitrogen
• Hydraulic Workover • Industrial Nitrogen
• Freezing • Hot Tapping • Gate Valve Drilling
RPC
Copyright 2007 Cudd Energy Services - An RPC, Inc. Company
www.cudd.com
10 Desta Drive, Ste. 420-E • Midland, TX 79705 • 432-570-5300

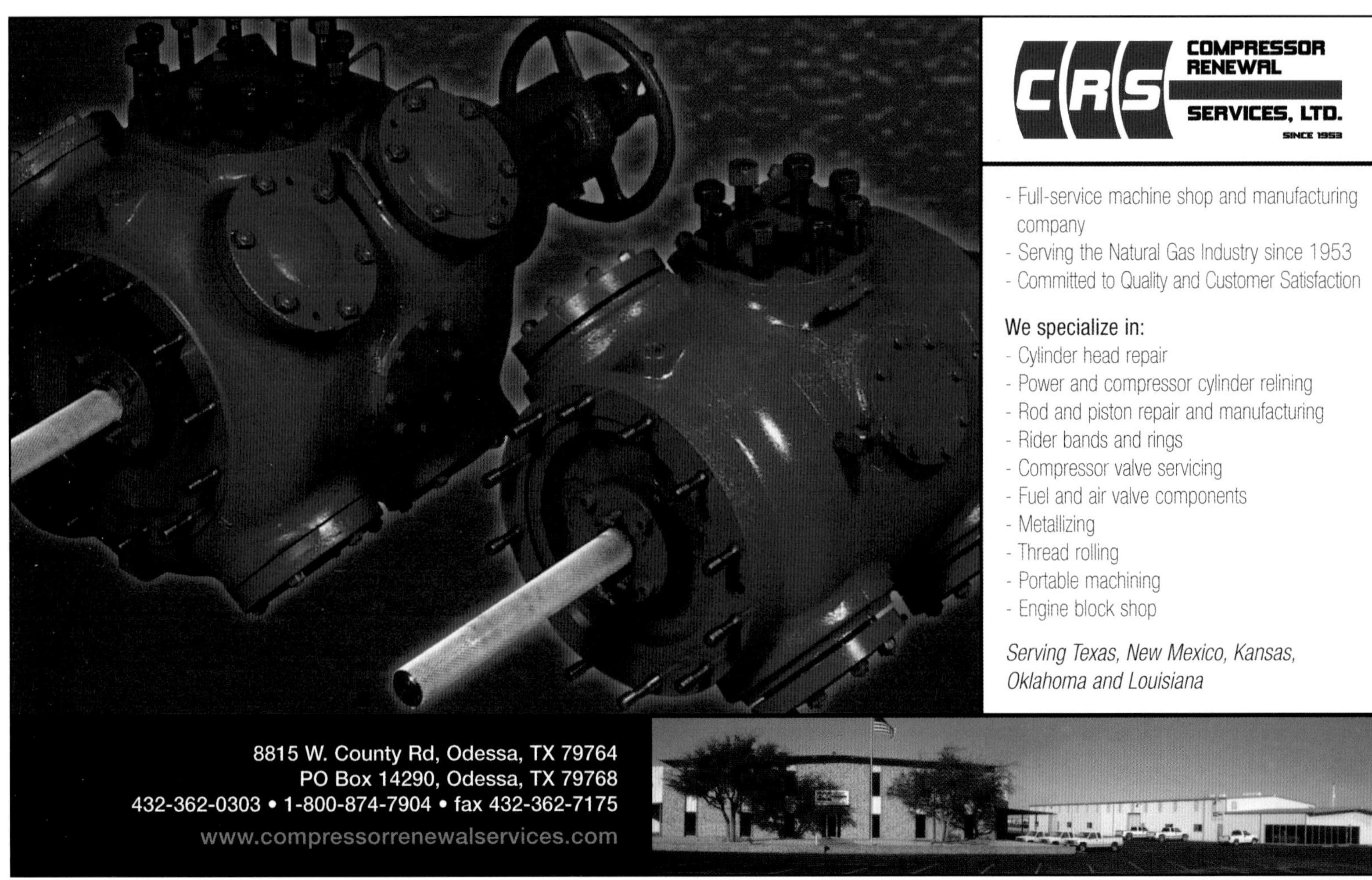
CRS
COMPRESSOR RENEWAL SERVICES, LTD.
SINCE 1953
- Full-service machine shop and manufacturing company
- Serving the Natural Gas Industry since 1953
- Committed to Quality and Customer Satisfaction
We specialize in:
- Cylinder head repair
- Power and compressor cylinder relining
- Rod and piston repair and manufacturing
- Rider bands and rings
- Compressor valve servicing
- Fuel and air valve components
- Metallizing
- Thread rolling
- Portable machining
- Engine block shop
Serving Texas, New Mexico, Kansas, Oklahoma and Louisiana
8815 W. County Rd, Odessa, TX 79764
PO Box 14290, Odessa, TX 79768
432-362-0303 • 1-800-874-7904 • fax 432-362-7175
www.compressorrenewalservices.com

CAREER HIGHLIGHTS

1954 Graduates from Texas A&M; volunteers for military draft

1957 After serving out military time, sells life insurance; forms partnership with John May that will evolve into Clajon Gas Co.

1964 Buys out John May's interests

1972 Purchases ranch in Alpine, TX

1973 Moves from Fort Stockton, TX to Midland, TX

1975 Williams's ultimately lucrative Gataga #2 gas well blows out

1975 Forms Williams Partnership; buys ranch in Belding, TX; forms Williams Ranches, launches registered purebred business with Brangus cattle

1976 Forms Williams Exploration

1978 Holds first of the famed Brangus sales at his Alpine ranch

1979 Clajon grows prodigiously from the Giddings boom (Austin Chalk play in South Texas)

1982 Clajon becomes the largest individually owned gas company in Texas

1982-1988 Teaches wildly popular entrepreneurship class at A&M with co-professor Dr. Ella Van Fleet

1979 Receives the Distinguished Service Award of the American Association of Petroleum Landmen

1981 Williams's companies reach 1,200 employees total (in 1972 there were only fifteen)

1981 Receives A&M's Distinguished Alumnus Award

1982 Named to the Forbes Four Hundred List

1983 Opens ClayDesta Plaza, a $42 million office park

1984 Forms ClayDesta Communications

1985 Sells off his purebred cattle just a few months before their market collapses

fourteen. For labor, he chose illegal immigrants from Mexico because they exhibited a better work ethic than his school peers. Williams enjoyed hanging out with his Mexican employees while they ate their sack lunches. He picked up a fair bit of Spanish by listening attentively to their chatter and song. This rapt attention undoubtedly endeared him to his workers. They understood what Williams felt: that the appreciation of mariachi music is "an appreciation of Mexican people and [their] culture."

When Williams finally tired of singing with the mariachis that night in 1964, he returned to his table. His three male buddies were abuzz, but not about Williams's performance. They had spotted two attractive young women at a nearby table and were anxious to combine parties. Sandy Hyde and her good friend Modesta were equally interested in making this a coed affair. After all, the girls had come to Monterrey Kitchen with merriment in mind. Earlier that evening they had wracked their brains to come up with a suitable excuse for celebration. Not having birthdays any time soon, the best they could come up with was Sandy's brother's adoption of a baby. Neither the brother, nor the baby, was there in Midland to be feted, but no matter. As Modesta puts it, "we were just looking for a cause to go out, have a cold beer and eat Mexican food."

Mariachi music is most often heard at celebrations, where its spirited beat complements the festival feel. But there's more to mariachi music than partying and *La Cucaracha*. The tradition holds a treasure trove of love songs, or *seranatas*, which originally functioned as love missives between young men and women. When social mores slackened and men and women were allowed to intermingle, *seranatas* became less necessary for courting. But that June night in 1964, Williams found that sometimes old-fashioned methods work best when wooing a woman. "He was the star of the show up there with the mariachi," recalls Modesta forty-three years later, still swooning at the memory.

From Ten to Two-Thousand A Day:

How Aghorn Barreled Forward

Frosty Gilliam, Jr., with wife Rhonda; son Matt; daughter Laura.

P.O. Box 12663
Odessa, TX 79768
432-550-0804

Aghorn Energy was started in 1987 by Frosty Gilliam, Jr. and his brother Tim. The company's name is a clever nod to the two founders' alma maters, Texas A&M and UT Austin. Frosty, an Aggie, graduated with a degree in Petroleum Engineering in 1980, while Tim graduated a few years later as a Longhorn in Journalism. Native Odessans, Tim and Frosty were familiar with West Texas and its industry. Their father, Frosty Gilliam, Sr., had been running a well-logging service called Temperature Evaluation Logging Company since 1975.

Aghorn's first purchase was in 1987 and consisted of a pair of wells for $90,000, the funds for which came from Frosty's and Tim's savings. The two wells produced a meager ten barrels a day. Frosty, who was living in Dallas during the company's creation, decided to move back to Odessa and more closely manage Aghorn's development. Remembers Frosty, "We were trying to build the company through acquisitions. We didn't drill because it was too risky and we had no money. Times were pretty tough back then…prices were pretty low. Majors wanted to sell, but it was tough to buy because we didn't know what oil prices would do." Frosty, Sr., watching his sons struggle with their fledgling business and observing the slowness of his own service company, offered Frosty some advice: either make a big effort to get Aghorn truly running or go back to work as an engineer.

Frosty, Jr. consulted with his wife Rhonda and they knew they needed to offer their concerns to God in prayer. "My wife's one of those people that likes to give God deadlines," jokes Frosty, "she was praying specifically for an answer by June 1, 1989. So I agreed with her for God to show us His will by then." As always, God was faithful and their prayer was answered. On the Friday before Memorial Day, Frosty received a call from Texaco saying Aghorn was the winning bidder of two leases. Still in awe today, Frosty marvels, "What was amazing was we weren't the highest bidder. We were the fifth highest, but the first four dropped out for no reason. God's hand was truly in that."

Frosty and Tim borrowed $225,000 from their father to buy the Texaco wells, which yielded thirty-five barrels a day. In eleven months, they were able to reimburse Frosty, Sr., with interest. Aghorn proceeded to develop slowly, just "picking up a few deals here and there," until October 1991 when the brothers acquired their first really big deal. After that, business set off at a steady clip. In 1996, Tim sold his shares to Frosty and retired – at thirty-three years old. The same year, Frosty formed a separate company, Aghorn Oil & Gas and invited Trent Day to be a partner. "Trent's been a real blessing and a tremendous asset to Aghorn. He's extremely capable – the best field person in West Texas," says Frosty appreciatively. He continues, chuckling, "We are extremely compatible and get along great. It's funny, both our wives are named Rhonda and our oldest children are both named Matt."

About Aghorn's business approach, Frosty expounds, "We buy production from other companies where we think we can operate it more efficiently. We operate real lean – ten employees: three in the office and seven in the field. We also have our own well-service rig and roustabout company that takes care of some of the day-to-day operations. We take pride in knowing our niche and that is to maximize production from existing well bores." Aghorn currently operates over 600 wells, ninety percent of which are located in Ector County. These wells, along with other Aghorn interests, produce approximately 2,000 barrels a day. When asked about his plans for Aghorn's future, Frosty beams, "I love my job. I think that I wouldn't want to do anything else, I don't plan on retiring. Our motto has always been, 'If your business is not growing, it's dying.'"

Today, Frosty and Trent are moving forward, having fun as they go. Frosty's brother Tim, by the way, is pursuing a PhD in Psychology at Texas A&M at Commerce. A Longhorn becoming an Aggie – now that just proves nothing's impossible for the Gilliam family.

1988 Reenters the cattle business, participates until 1995

May 8, 1987 Rides a horse up the Texas Capitol's steps to protest a bill that would deregulate AT&T

Jun 3, 1987 Woefully sells Clajon

1989 Merges ClayDesta Communications with an Atlanta-based corporation

1990 Wins GOP nomination for Texas Governor; narrowly loses race to Ann Richards

1994-1995 Cuts back on other businesses to refocus on Giddings play

1988 Inducted into the Hall of Honor of the Texas A&M Corps of Cadets

2001 Reclaims ClayDesta Plaza (which he had sold during previous financial straits); Williams's well Lee Fazzino #2 comes in with forty million cubic feet of gas a day

2004 Purchases Midland-based Southwest Royalties Inc.; Receives the Foy Proctor Memorial Cowman's Award of Honor from the Haley Museum

2005 Selected as Muster Speaker for the main campus of Texas A&M University

2006 Designated the Texas State Historical Association Businessman of the Decade

2007 Receives A&M's Kupfer Distinguished Executive Award

Jul 7, 2007 Fifty-year anniversary of being in the oil business

Aug 2007 Release of *Claytie: The Roller-Coaster Life of a Texas Wildcatter* by Mike Cochran, Texas A&M University Press (This thorough biography was a resource for this timeline.)

Oct 25, 2007 Receives Texas A&M Distinguished Agricultural Award

Nov 2007 Texas Business Hall of Fame Induction

Apr 2008 Receives Texas Parks & Wildlife Foundation Conservation Champion Award

Williams's posse mustered their courage and sidled over to the women. Introductions were breezily exchanged. Modesta remembers, "Claytie and I just locked on." To illustrate, she claps her palms together like they're a pair of powerful magnets. "The sparks kinda flew." Her eyes twinkle mischievously, indicating that "kinda" is an understatement. After the Monterrey Kitchen, the party proceeded to Modesta's apartment. The men and women lolled around for a while, then took their leave—all except Williams. Modesta mixed vodka and Kahlua into Black Russians for them both. Describing the nothing-but-liquor concoction, Modesta remarks matter-of-factly, "Very potent but good. I don't think I've had one since." Sipping their drinks, Williams and Modesta lay on their bellies, heads propped on hands, listening to music and looking at each other moonily. They talked and talked till the Black Russians lulled them to sleep on the living room carpet.

Williams is never paid for his services as an impromptu singer. In fact, more often than not, it is he who does the paying, reimbursing musicians for the privilege of joining in. Mariachi bands are typically impressed with Williams, who requests more obscure music than the gringo-favorites "Rancho Grande" and "La Cucaracha." Where Williams deviates from tradition is costume. He usually performs wearing whatever he came in with. On the rare occasion that he does accessorize, it's often with a nod to his alma mater. For example, while singing at one of his legendary ranch parties, he sported Aggie boots (underneath a Scottish kilt and sombrero, no less). But even comically dressed, Williams maintains a solemn respect for the Mexican art form. "The mariachi beat, rhythm, and spirit can't be imitated," declares the Aggie, "I'm pretty damn good for a gringo, but not near as good as they [are]."

Two weeks after the Black Russian incident, Williams rang up Modesta for a second date. "I wondered what

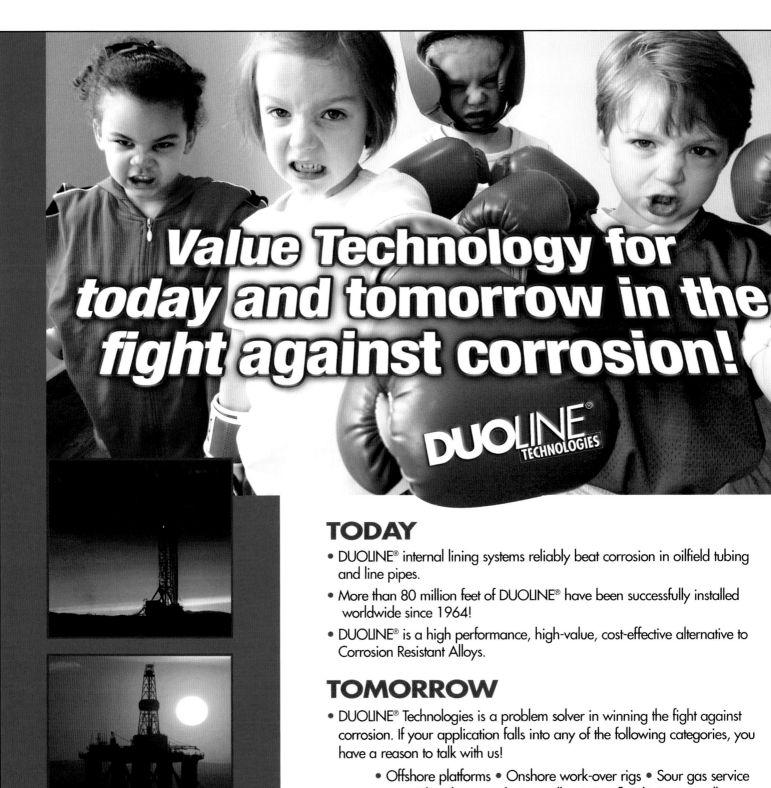

took him so long," reflects the former model. Then, a realization flashes across her face. "He probably had a date the next weekend with a different girl," she says wryly. When they began dating, Williams and Modesta were both jaded from failed first marriages. However, their wary attitude toward matrimony soon melted under the heat of their soul-connection. Williams elaborately proposed to Modesta on Valentine's Day in 1965; they married three months later.

The respect Williams exhibits toward Mexican-Americans is not limited to their music. As a young man, Williams ran for president of the Fort Stockton Jaycees. Among the issues spurring him to candidacy was the admittance of Mexican-Americans to the organization. Though Williams lost the presidential vote, his adamant support of prospective member Frank Velasco helped the Hispanic man gain entrance. The two men became lifelong friends. A few years later, Williams entrusted Velasco with the foremanship of his Fort Stockton farm.

Reflecting on "El Papalote," the mariachi song that helped capture Modesta's heart, Williams paraphrases, "I'm not a kite! No woman's gonna run my life!" Breaking into a toothy grin, he quickly adds, "but we all know that's not true!" And Williams knows better than anyone. As a newlywed, Modesta acquired the nickname "little eagle" for the talon-like fingernails she dug into her husband's shoulders whenever he got off course. It took many tempestuous rows and several nights spent in the caliche pit (West Texas's version of the proverbial "doghouse") for things to settle down. Today, man and wife still have their fiery temperaments, but they've learned to channel them into more constructive activities like trophy hunting and traveling the world.

"I make the living and she makes the living worthwhile."

The Williamses still speak some Spanish whenever their wanderlust takes them to Mexico, but Clayton's mariachi performances have become few and far between. The oilman doesn't seem disturbed by this decrease in singing. After all, mariachi music has already achieved the greatest end he could hope for: capturing Modesta's heart. Modesta radiates with joy when she considers her mate, "To still have that twinge when I see him come through the door—I'm happy! I still have that love for him. Not that first wow-crazy love, but it's still a strong happiness and love that I wish everybody could have." Williams, another inveterate softie, seconds his wife's thoughts, "I make the living and she makes the living worthwhile. We're an ongoing love story."

a family legacy of safety

JACK & LARRY FEELER

"Smilin'" Jack Feeler was a pipeline welder who loved life. As a young man, he followed family tradition by traveling the country, welding and doing plant fabrication. In 1940, he married Patti Nell Little, a fellow Odessan. Jack served in the military, started a family of five children, and continued his pipeline travels throughout the central United States.

In 1963, Jack opted for a job with roots. He and two partners, Bobby Brown and Junior Rogge, started **Three Way Constructors, Inc.**, which provided local pipeline construction, fabrication, and repairs. Their honest, hard work helped the company flourish. Soon, Three Way had hundreds of employees working all over the Permian Basin.

But there was a problem. By 1987, Jack's company, Three Way Constructors, found itself paying over a million dollars per year in worker's compensation insurance and claims. Jack always wanted the best care for his injured workers. He empathized with them because a welding rig had run over him in 1968, crushing a leg and puncturing a lung. Even so, Jack felt cheated by the many injury claims that seemed illegitimate. Jack turned to his youngest son, Larry, for advice. **Larry Feeler** is a licensed physical therapist and owner of the private practice Odessa Physical Therapy.

Larry and Jack devised a plan to conduct baseline medical testing for all Three Way new-hires. They screened for pre-existing problems that typically cost employers the most money, i.e., carpal tunnel, bad backs, torn knee ligaments, and shoulder muscle tears. Father and son also administered standardized lifting tests and required workers to safely demonstrate the essential duties of their job (digging, throwing skids, carrying calipers, etc.). From this screening, Jack and Larry were able to better match workers' strengths with their jobs to create a safer workplace. The first year, injuries and costs per claim were reduced over 60% and Three Way saved three-quarters of a million dollars!

Several other local oilfield businesses implemented the same tests with similar success. Soon, nearby towns like San Angelo, Abilene, and Lubbock were clamoring for the tests. By 1990, Larry and his partner, Christiana Robichaud, incorporated software to effectively track employee data. Furthermore, they built a work-simulation medical office with: an operating drilling rig, a well service platform, an 18-wheel simulator, automotive and construction stations, beverage distribution, digging areas, and hundreds of other job-specific tests. Their testing method was a breakthrough for the medical industry.

In 1994, Larry formally incorporated WORKSTEPS, which is currently the largest functional employee-testing company in the United States. WORKSTEPS' success has led to OVER ONE MILLION WORKERS TESTED nationwide for all-sized employers (including Fortune 500 and Fortune 100 companies) in every industry sector. The test is available in over 1,000 locations in 48 states.

Today hundreds of thousands of U.S. workers are safer, thanks to the influence and innovation of oil field entrepreneur Jack Feeler.

Were it not for his unexpected passing in 1999, Johnny Warren would have been featured like the other GIANTS in this book—with a two-page photo spread and interview-based feature. Unable to follow the same format, but still wanting to recognize Warren as a West Texas GIANT, we invited writer Ellen Hopkins to pen the following tribute.

In Honor of Johnny Warren

by Ellen Hopkins

Successful people often achieve notoriety among industry peers or recognition from competitors, but few climb the ladder without sacrificing some segment of a balanced life. Johnny Warren's family, friends and industry associates remember him as one who achieved balanced success by working hard and by playing hard, the latter involving his championship golf ability and favorite quail lease.

"Dad was never a workaholic, and he spent more time than anyone thought he had giving to church, community, family, and friends," said Stirling Warren. "That's probably the big thing I took from him is the importance of maintaining a balance all the way around."

Johnny Warren built Compressor Systems Inc. (CSI) into the founding brick of Warren Equipment Company, an umbrella including Warren CAT and Ignition Systems and Controls. In 1971, CSI was a subsidiary of Treanor Equipment Company located on Murphy Street in Odessa. Owned by Jack Treanor, the company supplied Caterpillar-related products to the industry and focused on short-term rental compression. Since the gas compressor business is technically demanding, Treanor surveyed oil and gas companies in Midland and Odessa for a general manager of the small subsidiary he wanted to grow.

"Johnny Warren's name was offered more often than anyone else," recalled Wayne Lutke, CSI retiree. "Johnny was an excellent choice with his University of Texas double degrees in petroleum engineering and business administration."

Treanor spun off CSI and its four employees, and placed Johnny as president. The company added another twenty-three employees within eighteen months, expanding into compressor fabrication, i.e., pairing gas compressors with correctly-matched engines, and selling these packages to companies producing natural gas in neighboring states.

"Johnny was very accessible, good to talk to, and he had a lot of plans," said Pete Torres, who began in 1971. "He was always telling us he had 'this' in mind, and we're going to do 'that.' He kept us well informed about his dream."

Frank Denena, Johnny's first employee, said Johnny had the ability to bring good people together to form the nucleus of the company. All the department heads would get together on Fridays in a downtown Odessa hotel to have lunch and talk business.

"When we worked on Murphy St., Johnny used to say he didn't want to be the world's biggest company; he just wanted to be the biggest and best company in the Permian Basin," said Denena. "Well, that didn't last long. He had to grow because he acquired so many customers."

Johnny foresaw a greater need in the Permian Basin for all types of compression – from wellhead to gathering system to gas processing plants – and he planned CSI's future accordingly.

"At the beginning, a manager has his hands on everything," said Denena. "Johnny soon named vice presidents and that freed him up to handle important things like financing. It takes a lot of money to buy the iron and keep up with payroll. Johnny stayed close and was always on top of things, but he let us take care of our day-to-day operations."

In 1975, Johnny opened an expanded facility near Terminal on Hwy. 1788, and consistently added regional service facilities wherever CSI's customer base grew. Denena said shortly after the move the company grew in leaps and bounds, and Johnny created a lot of jobs for people. Later in the year, Johnny bought CSI.

"Johnny's vision for the company was one of expansion," said Richard Folger, Warren Equipment Company president and CEO. "He was a true entrepreneur in every sense. He embraced opportunity and risk. The result is an enormously successful company."

It occurred to him that repairing some natural gas engine parts would increase quality so he established Ignition Systems and Controls (ISC) in 1981. And he made CSI a customer of other compressor manufacturers – Ariel, Worthington and Corken among them – pairing those models in CSI packages along with Caterpillar, White Superior and Waukesha engines.

"Johnny knew he had a superior product," said John Larsen, manager of Treanor Equipment Company's engine division. "He kept his standards high; he expected a lot of himself and from the rest of us. He instilled in us to treat our employees well, and in turn they would treat the customer well. He believed very strongly in this."

Stirling Warren said his dad was a visionary in that he could see raw talent in an employee and realize a way to develop it. He treated everybody with respect, from the custodian at CSI to the round table group he ate with at the Petroleum Club. He also had a knack for looking ahead six months, one year or two years down the road so he could be prepared.

"One of Dad's sayings was, *Prepare in the good times for the bad*," said Warren. "Dad was always grounded enough to know that bad times were waiting around the corner, so he planned ahead when times were good."

Times did take a bad turn in the early 1980s, not just within the industry but with a close personal relationship as well.

"Around 1982, the industry slowed down," said Lutke. "There comes a time when you can't change the fact that oil and gas prices have dropped and your customers no longer have need of any more new or rental compressors. It's just economics, and a company like CSI had to work through those times."

The next year, Jack Treanor was killed in a plane crash. His CAT dealership covered a 40-county area of West Texas.

"In late 1984, CAT selected Johnny as the new Dealer Principal of that area with some CSI stock pledged as collateral," explained Dwain McMillan, Treanor Equipment's promotion manager.

"The exciting roar of the engines, the clank of the steel…it was a good way to learn about the industry." GIANT Nick Taylor reflects on working as a roughneck

Photo courtesy of Hendershot Photography

"Johnny continued operations as Treanor Equipment Co. and he assumed the duties of president and CEO. With offices in Abilene and Odessa, the new dealership added more than 150 employees."

Johnny built upon Jack Treanor's twenty-seven-year reputation. He also relinquished his position as CSI's CEO, although he continued as chairman of the board and majority stockholder. His first challenge was to find a use for the industry equipment made idle by the 1980s downturn.

"Johnny was an unbelievable visionary," said Larson. "The mid-80s drilling bust left engine sales bleak, and there were banks going under and a lot of auctions of CAT engines. Johnny asked one day if we had ever thought of buying those engines at auction, refurbishing them in our shops and selling them to other industries. He said, 'Look, this power is just sitting out there. Somebody needs it. It's such a bargain; we just need to find a place to use it.'

"So we bought the equipment for five cents on the dollar and our salesmen tried to sell it for thirty cents on the dollar," continued Larson. "We kept our shops and our employees busy. We sold to all different industries in the world – from Del Monte banana growers in South Texas to locomotives, agricultural and construction businesses, and we converted engines for their needs. We became a large player in the used equipment business."

Charlie Berridge, twenty-eight-year company pilot, said Johnny's business savvy and demeanor brought respect from employees and industry peers.

"Although he never asked for respect, when he walked in a room he commanded respect just by his presence," said Berridge. "He acted the same and treated other people the same whether he just made a million dollars or had just lost a million. There was nothing false about him; what you saw was exactly who he was."

Folger said Johnny's appeal centered on a leadership quality that made people feel comfortable with him.

"One of the greatest compliments I ever heard or read about him," said Folger, "stated that you could be in a roomful of people with Johnny and no matter the reason for the gathering or why you were in attendance – whether you were leading the delegation or carrying the books – you would leave the room feeling that you were the most important person Johnny had talked to that day. That was one very special talent."

The 80s industry downturn culminated in 1986 when CSI's employment dropped from 1,200 down to about 250. Optimism continued fading as many people either left for non-petroleum-related jobs or were laid-off.

"We had some layoffs here and there, but many people quit because they didn't see a future in the industry," said David Murdock, CSI president and COO. "More than two hundred of us at CSI, however, were excited to be a part of the solution because of our loyalty to and trust in Johnny Warren."

Company focus shifted from a combination of production and service to one of primarily service.

"It wasn't long before the company quit building new units," remembered Jim Wilson. "But we had units in the field that still needed maintenance and units sent to the shop that needed refurbishing, so that's where we concentrated our efforts. A core group of those fabrication mechanics – long-time, loyal employees who were dedicated to CSI – were retrained as service mechanics."

Murdock, who has been with CSI since 1977, said he never saw Johnny waiver about the company's future and whether it would still be around fifty years down the road.

"Johnny never took his eye off his goal," said Murdock. "He had a clear, precise vision of what he wanted to accomplish and it excited him. There was no doubt in his mind that CSI would attain long-term success regardless of whether times were good or bad."

Expansion in 1986 included the purchase of West Texas Equipment Co., the CAT dealer for the Texas Panhandle. In 2002, Warren CAT purchased Darr Equipment and became the CAT dealer for all of Oklahoma. Colleagues attribute Johnny's success, optimism and foresight to some admirable self-education habits.

"He read three newspapers every morning including the Wall Street Journal," Larsen said. "He had a personal book and a business-related book going at all times, and he had a network of confidants from the Petroleum Club and the Country Club. He would listen to a lot of people in different industries, and then jot notes on his old yellow tablet. He knew the big players in the oil industry worldwide, and he understood why certain companies and different countries acted the way they did."

Warren CAT manager Scot McKinney said he remembers, "An older man in Midland checked me into a hotel late one night and noticed I worked at West Texas CAT. He asked if I knew Mr. Warren. I said, 'Yes, Sir, he's my boss.' And that man said to me, 'What a lucky guy.' Many years ago, he used to caddy for Johnny at Midland Country Club."

Johnny Warren died unexpectedly in 1999 at age sixty-three. Folger said Johnny's passion for his employees continues as part of his ongoing legacy and his habit of always putting others first.

"He began a company program to pay the cost for any employee who wants to further his education," said Folger. "He also established a scholarship program specifically to educate the sons and daughters of employees. Today, Warren Equipment Company continues to contribute significantly to a wide range of programs which center on education and improving the community."

Photo courtesy of Mark R. Swindler, Photographer

Advertisers Index